"This book . . . offers rigorous research on rural trends, demographics, and the subtleties of smallness; it motivates ministry in those areas with the gospel of grace; it equips you to develop a theological vision for the place of your calling; it immerses you in real stories of rural ministry; and it challenges urban ministry biases with winsome wit, but most of all it calls us to love in place and discover something more of the immeasurable love of God in Christ Jesus for all the world."

Jonathan Dodson, lead pastor of City Life Church, Austin, founder of gcdiscipleship.com, author of *The Unbelievable Gospel* and *Here in Spirit*

"This is a book whose time has come. I've long appreciated Stephen Witmer's advocacy for ministry in the small places. And now we have an apologetic, a theological vision for this particular work. He makes the case for small places without patronizing them or denigrating ministry in other areas. I even appreciated his pushback to the urban thesis of the early church. That's what makes this book an important read, even if you could never imagine living in the places where Stephen and I grew up."

Collin Hansen, editorial director for The Gospel Coalition, coauthor of *A God-Sized Vision: Revival Stories That Stretch and Stir*

"Stephen Witmer's latest book reminds me of my mom's Sunday dinners. The aroma of the well-prepared content drew me in, each savory mouthful deeply satisfied, and the lasting value has given me ongoing nourishment. I'm excited to invite church leaders from urban, suburban, and rural places to feast on this much-needed book. And like mom's Sunday meals, Stephen wrote the last chapter as a memorable dessert."

David Pinckney, pastor at River of Grace Church, Concord, New Hampshire, and codirector of Rural Collective Acts 29

"The gospel is not just about reaching the masses, it is about lost people wherever they may live. It is about God's value of the unimportant and insignificant. Stephen reminds us that if we abandon the rural places in our mission, then we do more than neglect the spiritual plight of rural people, we neglect the gospel itself. For this reason alone, this book is a must-read for all denominational leaders, seminary professors and students, and those who desire to serve in small towns and rural communities."

Glenn Daman, senior pastor, Rive  n, author of *The Forgotten Church*

D11159500

"*A Big Gospel in Small Places* is an incredible book that really answers core questions of why ministering in forgotten communities matters. In this book, Stephen Witmer offers very practical advice and compelling theological vision that should make us all consider preaching the gospel both in big and small places. This book should be read by all pastors."

Robert Manda, codirector of Rural Collective Acts 29, pastor of New Life Church, Malawi, Africa

"What a long-awaited, welcomed book! What rare, refreshing, and compelling insights that validate the selfless investments faithful men and women—my heroes—are making in places that some consider unstrategic. Thank you, Stephen Witmer, for stirring our thinking and quickening our hearts for mighty gospel-oriented work in small places!"

Ron Klassen, executive director of RHMA (Rural Home Missionary Association)

"What a breath of fresh air to understand the gospel as motivator and as the approach to ministry! That's exactly what Stephen Witmer helps us understand in *A Big Gospel in Small Places*. Clear, passionate, and biblical, Witmer's book lays a foundation for ministry that is rooted in the nature and content of the gospel. . . . Stephen's call is to flesh out the gospel in whatever location or ministry God has called us to. This book will be extremely valuable for anyone in or considering ministry, and it is not just for those in small, forgotten places. But what an encouragement it will be for them! As director of Village Missions, a ministry that serves the forgotten places of rural America, I can't wait to start using and promoting this book!"

Brian S. Wechsler, executive director of Village Missions

"Jesus is for everyone everywhere. Unfortunately, the lure of big cities and their amenities seduces many into feeling the need to plant and pastor churches in areas where there's a perception that a bigger opportunity to reach the lost exists. In the meantime, our small and rural towns have been left behind. In this book my brother Stephen presents us with an amazing opportunity to check our hearts and become intimately informed about the needs of our brothers and sisters in these all-too-often forgotten places."

Belafae Johnson, pastor of Purposed Church, Mascoutah, Illinois

"Stephen shows how every place, no matter the size, needs the gospel. This book provides a theological foundation and shows the importance of ministry in rural America. And not only does Stephen provide this theological foundation but he also gives practical ways to do ministry in smaller communities and places. As a pastor of a rural church and a supporter and planter of small-town churches across the country, this is one of the few books on small-town ministry that truly provides insight into what it means to take the gospel to villages and towns."

Michael Houle, small town specialist Vineyard USA, Multiply Vineyard, senior pastor, Valley Vineyard Church

"Stephen Witmer has written an accessible, experiential, and theologically rich book. It's a vital read. Drawing on the latest research and tapping into the abiding treasures of the Scriptures, Witmer challenges the prevailing missiological trend to prioritize the city. He calls rural and small-town leaders to 'love deeply what God loves perfectly.' This is Witmer's rallying cry, and it rings true. It's time for the rural church, from its unique vantage, to point the way for the church universal to reclaim its cruciform message, question the prevailing metrics of success, and embrace its vocation to become, in Witmer's apt phrase, 'see-through to the gospel.'"

Brad Roth, pastor of the West Zion Mennonite Church, Moundridge, Kansas, author of *God's Country*

"We need churches wherever there are people. My friend Stephen Witmer has written a very useful book on how Christians can minister fruitfully in small places. This book is rooted in a robust, gospel-centered theological vision that helps Christians to disentangle their value from any particular zip code, whether in a city or in a small town. I found the last chapter on the reasons for prioritizing big-place ministries to be a gracious response to the urban apologetic."

Stephen T. Um, senior pastor of Citylife Presbyterian Church of Boston, author of *Micah for You*

"As someone who has written a book on small-town ministry and has spent countless hours speaking on small-town ministry and coaching small-town pastors, I highly recommend this book. Whether you are considering the importance and validity of small-town ministry or currently in the trenches loving and leading people in small towns, you need to read this. It's encouraging, helpful, accessible, thoughtful, and clear. Great work, Stephen!"

Donnie Griggs, author of *Small Town Jesus*

"Stephen Witmer's *A Big Gospel in Small Places* is compelling because it is a simple depiction of the deeply normal, deeply human life of small places, a life that many evangelicals have regarded with indifference for far too long. For several decades now, evangelicals have thought more often in terms of size, efficiency, and influence than in the more humane and Christian terms of fidelity, affection, and rootedness. There is a call in this book to love small places and serve them faithfully, of course. But there is also a call to cultivate a certain patience in one's own life, a commitment to belong fully to the local life of one's home place, and to view all of this work with a smiling affection borne of the confidence that God smiles on such a life. This is an exceptional book and one that I am happy to commend to others."

Jake Meador, author of *In Search of the Common Good*, editor in chief of Mere Orthodoxy

"With *A Big Gospel in Small Places*, Stephen Witmer shows himself to be an important voice in a welcomed trend of finally giving small towns, and ministry in them, the attention they have long deserved. This is a thorough look at the needs, blessings, and challenges of small-town ministry from someone who knows his subject well, refuses to idealize it, takes on the challenges with open eyes, and calls us to engage these towns and churches with all of our hearts and minds."

Karl Vaters, author of *Small Church Essentials*

"Francis Schaeffer observed that there are no little people in God's sight and no little places: 'To be wholly committed to God in the place where God wants him—this is the creature glorified.' There is a tendency these days to quantify the value of ministry. This thinking assumes that bigger is better. The larger the population is, the greater the need. Such a view tends to rule out small places. Stephen Witmer helps us to correct this by showing us that small places are much like everywhere else. They are also different. Witmer makes an informed and winsome case for the importance of doing ministry in the places that many of us are inclined to overlook. *A Big Gospel in Small Places* will help you to understand not only the need but the unique nature of today's forgotten communities."

John Koessler, professor of applied theology and church ministry, Moody Bible Institute

A

BIG
GOSPEL

IN SMALL PLACES

(Why Ministry in Forgotten
Communities Matters)

Stephen Witmer

Foreword by Ray Ortlund

An imprint of InterVarsity Press
Downers Grove, Illinois

InterVarsity Press
P.O. Box 1400, Downers Grove, IL 60515-1426
ivpress.com
email@ivpress.com

InterVarsity Press® is the book-publishing division of InterVarsity Christian Fellowship/USA®, a movement of students and faculty active on campus at hundreds of universities, colleges, and schools of nursing in the United States of America, and a member movement of the International Fellowship of Evangelical Students. For information about local and regional activities, visit intervarsity.org.

Scripture quotations, unless otherwise noted, are from The Holy Bible, English Standard Version, copyright © 2001 by Crossway Bibles, a division of Good News Publishers. Used by permission. All rights reserved.

While any stories in this book are true, some names and identifying information may have been changed to protect the privacy of individuals.

Cover design and image composite: David Fassett
Interior design: Daniel van Loon
Images: red push pin: © Reinhard Weber / EyeEm / Getty Images
        city map: © FrankRamspott / Digital Vision Vectors / Getty Images

ISBN 978-0-8308-4155-4 (print)
ISBN 978-0-8308-5549-0 (digital)

Printed in the United States of America ∞

InterVarsity Press is committed to ecological stewardship and to the conservation of natural resources in all our operations. This book was printed using sustainably sourced paper.

Library of Congress Cataloging-in-Publication Data
Names: Witmer, Stephen E., 1976- author.
Title: A big gospel in small places : why ministry in forgotten communities matters / Stephen Witmer.
Description: Westmont, Illinois : InterVarsity Press, 2019. | Includes bibliographical references.
Identifiers: LCCN 2019029468 (print) | LCCN 2019029469 (ebook) | ISBN 9780830841554 (paperback) | ISBN 9780830855490 (ebook)
Subjects: LCSH: Missions. | Rural churches.
Classification: LCC BV2063 .W54 2019 (print) | LCC BV2063 (ebook) | DDC 253.09173/4—dc23
LC record available at https://lccn.loc.gov/2019029468
LC ebook record available at https://lccn.loc.gov/2019029469
A catalog record for this book is available from the Library of Congress.

P 25 24 23 22 21 20 19 18 17 16 15 14 13 12 11 10 9 8 7 6 5 4 3 2 1

Y 39 38 37 36 35 34 33 32 31 30 29 28 27 26 25 24 23 22 21 20 19

For my parents,

Daryl and Mary Witmer,

who have modeled for me a lifelong love for God

and a fruitful ministry in a small place

Contents

Foreword

RAY ORTLUND

I T IS WRITTEN, "Whoever exalts himself will be humbled, and whoever humbles himself will be exalted" (Matthew 23:12). Jesus said that, and he did not mean it as a mere ideal. Humility is, in fact, how human realities actually work. Pride cuts against the grain of God's creation. Pride is like trying to get healthy on junk food or trying to go home by the wrong road. Humility is the secret key to everything gloriously human.

John Calvin thought his way back over one thousand years of Christian thought and noticed what mattered most to two of our greatest saints:

> A saying of Chrysostom's has always pleased me very much, that the foundation of our philosophy is humility. But that of Augustine pleases me even more: " . . . so if you ask me concerning the precepts of the Christian religion, first, second and third and always I would answer humility."

Three hundred years later Charles Simeon, an Anglican minister writing to a friend, identified the heart of Christian ministry:

> Another observation of yours has not escaped my remembrance—the three lessons which a minister has to learn: 1. Humility. 2. Humility. 3. Humility. How long are we learning the true nature of Christianity!

Moving forward to the twentieth century, we read in C. S. Lewis what he has to say about pride, the worst thing about us:

According to Christian teachers, the essential vice, the utmost evil, is pride. Unchastity, anger, greed, drunkenness, and all that are mere fleabites in comparison. It was through pride that the devil became the devil. Pride leads to every other vice. It is the complete anti-God state of mind.

Historic Christianity agrees that humility is the only human condition God can bless. God himself said,

I dwell in the high and holy place,
    and also with him who is of a contrite and lowly spirit,
to revive the spirit of the lowly,
    and to revive the spirit of the contrite. (Isaiah 57:15)

All grandiosity offends God, especially ministry grandiosity. But all humility pleases God, especially ministry humility. We who serve the Lord are following an egoless nobody named Jesus who had no itch for prominent big-deal-ness. He is why small towns can be ideal settings for God's greatest blessings.

I am not proposing that large cities are for arrogant pastors and small towns are for humble pastors. If only virtue were as easily attainable as a rural zip code! But I am noticing how consistent a modest ministry location is with the display of the glory of Jesus, who was despised and rejected by this world's elite people. Doesn't his gospel flip all our values so that we are learning to say, "Let the lowly brother boast in his exaltation, and the rich in his humiliation" (James 1:9-10)? Small town ministry is not something to settle for. To quote the author of this wonderful book, "Strategic isn't always what we think."

Stephen Witmer understands the ironies God has built into his strategies for us all. In writing *A Big Gospel in Small Places*, Pastor Witmer knows what he's writing about—and where he's writing about. Serving Christ in a small Massachusetts town, as Stephen does, his ministry is a large kingdom commitment and an advantageous kingdom location. You doubt that? If we are honest, sometimes we do. But then we remember: Jesus came not from Rome, not even from Jerusalem, but from Nazareth, the equivalent to a small Massachusetts town of today. And even in glory above, right now our risen Lord still thinks of himself as a small-town man: "I am Jesus of Nazareth" (Acts 22:8). *A Big Gospel in Small Places* helps all of us to think with our Lord's categories and thus to think more deeply, ironically, wisely, and cheerfully about the where and, even more, about the Who of our gospel ministries.

If Christ has called you to serve him, then the location of your ministry is none of your business. You just follow his call. Wherever he leads you, your life will be forever glorious because he can put his glory anywhere. To quote Francis Schaeffer, "With God, there are no little people, no little places." What matters is not the size of our city or town but our consecration to the Lord in that city or town.

Wherever the Lord has called you, however modest in terms of this world, you can rejoice that he is the King of low places made strategic by his great plan. As you journey toward his celestial city, *A Big Gospel in Small Places* will help you keep on and keep on and keep on. And if the Lord has called you to a prominent place, this book will help you respect the churches in small places as equally significant in the eyes of Christ.

And all of us will humbly agree together, "Let the one who boasts, boast in the Lord" (1 Corinthians 1:31).

Introduction

THIS BOOK IS WRITTEN to address a massive reality and an urgent need. More than three billion people around the world today—nearly half the world's population—live in rural areas. Many others live in small, forgotten towns. And many of these people do not know Jesus. Their communities are often remote and underresourced. It can be difficult to go to such humble places, and difficult to stay. But if these billions of souls are to be reached with the gospel, we must go. In this book I'll make the case that the gospel isn't just the message we take to small places; it's our <u>motivation</u> for going to them in the first place and our means of fruitful ministry once we get there. We'll discuss these big realities soon enough; for now I'll begin (appropriately enough) with something quite small—the story of my own awakening to the needs and opportunities of small places.

I grew up in Monson, Maine (population 700), on the shores of Lake Hebron. Monson wasn't just small—it was remote. I rode a school bus half an hour each way to middle school and high school. The nearest mall and cinema were over an hour away. We lived, quite literally, on the edge of the wilderness. The Appalachian Trail passed through town, and between Monson and the northern end of the Trail lay the 100-Mile Wilderness. That meant all the hikers preparing for the seven-day trek north rested and resupplied in Monson. Because our neighbor ran the main hiker hostel in town, I grew up meeting larger-than-life personalities: people like Tuba Man, who walked the entire trail carrying his supplies in the bell of his instrument. Though the pungent odor of hikers permeated the air throughout the summer months, we were thankful for the income they generated for the Monson economy. We needed all the help we could get. Monson had a general store, an elementary school, a post office, a couple of churches, a penny-candy store and antiques seller, a small restaurant, a pizza place, a town museum, a laundromat, a gas station, a volunteer fire department, and a public library. That was about it.

My father pastored one of Monson's two churches. He and my mother had moved to Maine before starting a family, attracted by its beauty and isolation and eager to do ministry. My father took a three-church parish and for years preached every Sunday morning in three churches in three towns. The church in our hometown, the Monson Community Church, met in a white-steepled building with beautiful stained-glass windows. Attendance swelled to fifty in the summer thanks to an influx of hikers and the seasonal migratory patterns of retirees. There wasn't much turnover in the town or church. I grew up surrounded by the same church members who had changed my diaper.

There was a lot to like about Monson. Norm's Store offered an enticing selection of penny candy. Lake Hebron was a good place to swim and canoe. The surrounding woods were a delight to explore, and every winter we cut a Christmas tree from the hill overlooking the town. My brothers and I claimed the street in front of our house as a playground, stepping off only for the occasional passing car (mildly annoyed that the driver had the audacity to make us move). There were colorful characters like the dog catcher who styled himself as a police officer and the town manager who always had a cigar in the corner of his mouth. If you kept your ears open, you'd hear marvelous stories. Two local teen boys made a practice of switching lanes whenever they met each other driving opposite directions on the road. One particular day, one boy switched lanes and the other didn't. They collided head-on, but both walked away unharmed.

Somewhere along the way I began to grow restless. No one ever told me Monson was too small, too backwater, too isolated. No one ever openly encouraged me to leave. But at some point in my teen years I knew I would. Success, in my view, looked like getting away. As high school graduation neared, I poured over promotional material from colleges and developed an unofficial success ranking in my own mind. Classmates who stayed local came in at the bottom; those accepted at in-state universities were slightly higher, bettered by those who made it to a college further away in New England. The real successes were those who moved to a different part of the country altogether. In fact, I came to view my own success in life as directly proportional to the distance from home I moved and the size of the place where I lived. The further away and bigger the better.

The most noteworthy feature of this attitude was that it wasn't all that noteworthy. Somehow, without explicit prompting, I had bought into a culturally prevalent disdain for small places and the view that leaving was the trajectory of the bright and promising. This cultural narrative, developed and promoted by people I did not know, in places I had never been, was powerful enough to blind me to the treasures of the place I had known and experienced all my life.

I soon began to make good on my aspiration to get away. I attended college in suburban Wheaton, Illinois; lived for two years in downtown Minneapolis; and then pursued graduate studies on the North Shore of Boston and in Cambridge, England. I lived far from home in well-known, wealthy, historic places. I attended large urban and suburban churches very unlike the tiny rural church of my childhood. I was drawn to the excitement, energy, and resources of these churches, to the well-known and skilled preachers who filled their pulpits, to the energetic college students and educated young professionals who filled their buildings. These churches were admired and emulated by others. They had big budgets, big buildings, and lots of events. I enjoyed being at the center of things. In fact, I began to take pride in it. The important places where I was living made *me* feel important. Throughout my twenties, as I studied for the ministry, I dreamed of pastoring a large city-center church. My résumé—ministry experience with college students and young professionals and advanced degrees in New Testament studies—seemed to point in that direction.

But life is full of surprising turns. For more than a decade now I have been, as my father was before me, the pastor of a small church in a small place. There have been seasons of heartache, fear, longing, and pain—but I have loved it.

My church, Pepperell Christian Fellowship, is a nondenominational church on Main Street in the town of Pepperell, Massachusetts, an hour northwest of Boston and just minutes from the New Hampshire border. You've probably never heard of Pepperell. It's not a place people travel to so much as one they travel through. It's a former mill town of twelve thousand people with a rural vibe. There are abundant horse farms, numerous fruit and vegetable stands, excellent fly fishing, and no stop lights. Each year in the Fourth of July parade a fleet of gleaming, refurbished tractors chugs up Main Street. One summer not long ago, a moose ambled through town (that was, admittedly, unusual!). When I step outside my front door at night, it's dark and quiet, and I can see the stars. Few cars drive past. Once, on my way back across the street from our mailbox late at night, I lay down in the middle of the road just to see what it would feel like.

As a small-church, small-town pastor, I do some things that high-profile pastors of big churches in big places probably don't do. I once disposed of a decaying squirrel that had crawled into our old education building and then died. (Seminary did *not* prepare me for that.) My church recruits a snow-shoveling team to clear the steps and decks during the long New England winters; I'm an able-bodied adult and I live near the church, so I'm on that team. Sometimes when I'm moving tables or chairs, hanging a sign on Main Street, or doing some other mundane task with my friend and fellow pastor Jeff, we'll jokingly identify the nature of what we're doing with a social media hashtag. #SmallTownPastor!

The truth is that before coming to Pepperell, I wasn't trying to get to a small town. I hadn't experienced a dramatic change in my understanding of ministry. I hadn't suddenly felt a pressing burden for small places. On the contrary, it was God's clear, unexpected call to one particular small-town church that has slowly, sometimes painfully, led to a change in my understanding of ministry and place and to a passion for seeing small places reached with the gospel.

A decade in Pepperell has led me to rethink, refeel, and reimagine some things. It has caused me to reexamine the Bible, seeking to root my views, feelings, and aspirations in the gospel rather than in what I've absorbed from popular culture. It's forced me to reckon with personal pride and ambition as well as my long-time acceptance of some questionable understandings of city and country.

I've also realized that in going from big to small I've been swimming against not just the current of my own aspirations but that of evangelicalism, which seems to be increasingly prioritizing city ministry. In the past several decades, evangelicals have responded to the massive needs and opportunities created by a major shift of worldwide populations into urban areas.[1] In the 1970s the Southern Baptist Convention focused more intently on planting urban and ethnic churches and saw a major increase in the number of those churches, from one thousand congregations among ethnic groups in 1970 to 2,074 in 1980.[2] Throughout the 1980s the Lausanne Committee on World Evangelization sponsored numerous consultations in urban centers around the world. In 1989, Tim Keller moved to Manhattan to plant Redeemer Presbyterian Church, which grew rapidly and launched Redeemer City to City, a church-planting ministry that aims to start gospel movements in cities. More recently, the North American Mission Board of the Southern Baptist Convention has prioritized urban church planting through its strategy of focusing on thirty-two Send Cities, cities "with the greatest spiritual need and potential influence throughout North America." This is just a small sampling of an increasingly urban ministry focus. Observers have noticed a massive shift from suburban planting to urban planting in recent years. One writer notes that "since the 1990s, evangelicals have increasingly focused on 'strategic' church planting in elite centers of cultural impact" and that "emerging evangelicalism [has] a decidedly urban focus and feel."[3] An urban church planter says, "Everyone's planting in the heart of the city."[4]

Well, not me. My life has gone a different direction, and ministry in a small town has stirred deep desires in me. I want to know how best to reach the small place where God has sent me. I want to better understand its unique opportunities and be more equipped to do something about its unique challenges. I want to care more about this place and its people than I already do. Small-town ministry (like ministry anywhere) is *hard*. Over the past decade I've agonized with hurting people, puzzled how to help struggling people, and felt anxiety about angry people. So I want to know that what I'm doing counts. I want to know deep in my bones that it's not a waste for me to minister on the periphery in this small, unknown town rather than in the center of things in a great city. I want to understand the evangelical prioritizing of the city and how my small-town ministry fits in.

Is it true that the apostle Paul and other early Christian missionaries focused exclusively on city ministry, entirely avoiding the countryside? If so, did they do so for strategic reasons, believing that if the gospel captured the influential cities it would eventually spread to the surrounding small towns and countryside? If so, is this strategy of establishing urban beachheads also the most effective method for our own day and culture? Does the Bible teach that the world began in a garden (Eden) and will end in a city (the new Jerusalem)—and if so, is that end-time urban future a reason for me to devote my life to city ministry in the present? Though I've heard and read people I deeply respect making all these points as part of a case for prioritizing city ministry in our day, I've never seen a careful, probing assessment of these claims. I hope that will be one contribution of this book.

My deep desire to understand and appreciate the importance of the small-place ministry God has called me to has led me to seek out other small-place ministers in order to learn from their experiences. Over the past several years I've been challenged and inspired by small-town and rural pastors and Christian workers from the coalfields of West Virginia to the plains of Wyoming, from the valleys of Wales to the countryside of Ireland and the villages of northern Uganda. I've corresponded and prayed and worshiped and partnered with churches and pastors who are changing their small communities in North Carolina, Georgia, Texas, and Pennsylvania. Closer to home, a couple of friends and I have launched Small Town Summits, an initiative that seeks to resource and encourage those who minister in the small places of our region. As we've gathered with small-town laypeople, ministry leaders, and pastors from all over New England, we've learned of the struggles faced by those who pour their lives into tiny places. We've also been amazed by the choice servants God has called to largely forgotten and spiritually hardened villages and hamlets.

While I've learned a lot, it turns out my experience in small-town ministry hasn't so much resulted in the discovery of things I didn't know as in the *re*discovery of things I once knew. I've

come to see afresh the beauty and brokenness of small places—
the one in which I now live as well as others around the world and
throughout history. I've slowly come to view these places through
a biblical lens, with a gospel-centered theological vision, more like
God sees them. I long to communicate this vision in this book.

THE PLAN OF THIS BOOK

In the pages that follow I'll seek to answer three questions that
correspond with the book's three main sections. First, what are
small places like? Second, how can we minister fruitfully in small
places? Third, should I minister in a small place?

Place matters; hence the first question. One of the necessary
building blocks of a theological vision for small-town and rural
ministry is considering the promise and problems of these places.
It's important for us to recognize the features of small-place life
and culture we can enthusiastically embrace as well as those we
must necessarily challenge.

I'll address the second question (How can we minister fruitfully in a small place?) in the book's central section. We must
begin with the simple confidence that small-place ministry is not
a waste or something to be ashamed of. In fact, God calls some of
his brightest and most capable servants to minister in small, forgotten places for their whole lives. Church history is full of examples (some of which we'll examine in this book).

Sadly, some ministers in small places feel that they're smaller
people because of where they minister—that they're on the junior
varsity team, not good enough to make it in the exciting, influential places. They're envious, lonely, and restless, always wondering what they're missing. They spy on the ministries of others
(often on social media) instead of savoring their own. As a result,
their joy is diminished and their congregations are damaged. To
minister effectively in small places, we need a gospel-shaped
theological vision to see both ourselves and our places as God

does. As the gospel helps us disentangle our value from our postal code and the worth of our postal code from its size, amenities, and influence, we'll be freed for joyful gospel ministry right where we live. Practical small-place ministry suggestions are important, and we'll certainly get to them. But if they don't flow from a coherent theological vision, they'll just be additional burdens for insecure rural ministers to bear—or more trophies for prideful rural ministers to display.

The third big question (Should I minister in a small place?) is important for both current and would-be ministers to ask and answer. Perhaps this is a good place to make a couple of things clear. First, I won't try to persuade anyone to become a small-place minister. On the contrary, I'll make the case that many should *not*. I'm overjoyed that God is moving in the great cities and sprawling suburbs of the world, and I hope many more people will hear and obey his call to the big places. The last thing I want to do is persuade someone God has equipped and called to a city or suburb to go to the country instead.

Second, I won't argue that small-town and rural ministry is more important than city or suburban ministry. My friend Stephen Um, who cowrote *Why Cities Matter*, pointed out that he didn't title his book *Why Cities Matter More*. My own journey hasn't led me to believe that ministry in cities and suburbs is less important. Some of my dearest friends are pastors in big cities, and I've benefited from many conversations with them. Making a case for rural ministry needn't (and shouldn't) involve the denigration of ministry in bigger places.

But neither is small-place ministry *less* important than big-place ministry. God is calling some future ministers (perhaps currently leading a small group or faithfully serving in their church, maybe doing office work or plumbing or carpentry or engineering) to give their lives to God's great glory in small, forgotten places. Sadly, some simply will not hear that call. Some are unable even to imagine small-place ministry as an option. Others will dismiss the call because small-place ministry seems so unstrategic and undesirable. Still others will reluctantly accept the call, disappointed that a small church in a small place is their only option. They'll regard it as a training ground for something better and will therefore never give it their best.

It's not my goal to persuade anyone to go to small places. Rather, I hope to persuade everyone to be open to God persuading them to go to small places. If God isn't calling you to a rural ministry, please don't go to one. But if he *is* calling you to rural ministry, I long for you to respond with a joyful yes and then stay as long as he wants you there.

YOU

If you're ministering as a pastor, lay leader, or congregation member in a small place, I'm writing for you. I want to encourage you to press on in your ministry with deep satisfaction, purpose, and joy, and I'm praying for you as I write.

Much of this book has grown out of reflecting on the American context. That's due to my own location and limitations, not because I consider it more important. You may be a rural pastor or church member in Guatemala, Italy, India, or Ethiopia. I invite you to consider carefully your own place and context using the categories and approach I employ in part one and to draw deeply on parts two and three (which will be directly relevant for you) as you develop a small-place theological vision. I hope this book will be helpful, encouraging, and motivating for small-place churches and ministers all over the world.

Perhaps you sense a call to future small-place ministry. I'm writing for you as well. I hope this book will open you to the possibility of a call you might otherwise have rejected out of hand. Or, if God leads you to city or suburban ministry, I hope he will use this book to grow in you a greater appreciation for ministry in small, forgotten places.

I've tried also to write a book that will be helpful for those who are currently ministering in cities and suburbs. I hope you'll find that I value and rejoice in your call and that you'll also be helped to see the importance of the work being done by God's servants in smaller places. I hope my probing of the evangelical prioritization of city ministry will encourage you to weigh the evidence for yourself so that your call to bigger places is grounded on solid biblical foundations. Many city ministers serve small churches in parts of the city that, though urban, nonetheless have many elements of *small* about them. Though their cities may be famous, these ministers and their churches are not. If that's you, I believe much of what you'll read in this book will be relevant to you.

Wherever we do gospel work, fruitful ministry will flow from treasuring God and his gospel. It will be empowered by the Holy Spirit and sourced from the Bible, with deep, enduring roots. It will embody the very characteristics of the gospel it proclaims.

PART 1
WHAT ARE THE SMALL
PLACES LIKE?

(Small places are better and worse than we think)

1

Taking a Fresh Look at Small Places

SINCE 2016, there's been an increased curiosity about rural areas and small towns in the United States—the parts of the country largely responsible for the election of President Donald Trump.[1] The current curiosity is mainly from those who live in the big places, the cultural centers, and the major cities, and it generally runs along the lines of "Who *are* these people who voted for Trump? And *why* did they vote for him?" A flood of articles about rural America and its problems have appeared in the *Washington Post*, *Wall Street Journal*, *New York Times*, and other publications. J. D. Vance's memoir *Hillbilly Elegy*, about his roots in small-town Appalachia, has become a bestseller. Academic researchers, such as Princeton sociologist Robert Wuthnow, have been busy trying to explain rural America to the rest of the nation.

The renewed interest in small places isn't limited to the United States. On June 23, 2016, the United Kingdom voted for Brexit (the withdrawal of the UK from the European Union). Voters in small places influenced the result: more than half of voters in the English countryside chose to leave the European Union while big cities throughout the UK voted to remain. Commentators drew parallels between the influence of rural American and British voters.[2] And once again, similar questions were raised: who are these people, what do they care about, and why did they vote as they did? Other commentators have drawn attention to a strong urban-rural divide in Europe and the ways that divide has contributed to heated debates about immigration and to the increasing influence of nationalistic politics.[3]

THREE REALITIES OF THE RENEWED INTEREST IN SMALL PLACES

For the time being, the city mouse is more curious about his odd country cousin. The Trump election, the Brexit vote, and the subsequent fascination with the small places represent a significant turn of events.

This phenomenon reflects massive global shifts. Until recently in human history, there was no particular fascination with small places simply because almost *every place* was a small place. In 1800, more than 90 percent of the world's population lived in rural areas. To understand *rural*, you could simply talk to your neighbors or reflect on your own experience. Even after the global migration to cities accelerated, the countryside was still important enough that it wasn't usually deeply misunderstood or altogether forgotten. Rural and small-town life has been the main reality for most of the world for most of its history. No longer.

The renewed interest in small places presents a unique gospel opportunity. Despite rapid worldwide urbanization, the global rural population is currently about 3.4 billion people, nearly half the world's population.[4] I wrote much of this book in Northern Ireland, where my wife's family lives: around 37 percent of Northern Ireland's population is rural. Rural England has a population of around ten million—about 19 percent of the overall population.[5] New England, where my family and I live, has many rural areas with tremendous spiritual needs. A 2017 Barna study on the spiritual landscape of New England found "a movement that is quietly revitalizing Christianity in the diverse urban centers of New England, while the broader population of New England remains unreached and spiritually adrift."[6]

This is true the world over: many rural people do not know Jesus. This means that if the nations are to be reached with the gospel, followers of Jesus can't stay in the cities and suburbs. We must venture into and minister long-term in the small, forgotten places. Perhaps the current interest of our broader culture will spark curiosity among those who long to bring gospel hope wherever there are people. Encouragingly, since 2016 there's been increased evangelical interest in rural areas and small towns. Numerous articles and some excellent books and conferences are calling for rural church planting and renewal efforts. Several new rural ministries and networks have formed (including Small Town Jesus and the Acts 29 Rural Collective), and there's been increased visibility for organizations like the Vineyard's Small Town USA initiative, the Rural Home Missionary Association, and Village Missions.

But most likely the renewed interest from our broader culture will not last. The fascination will fade as the 2016 election grows more distant and the national media focuses on other matters. While the current cultural interest regarding small places is indeed a gospel opportunity, it is only an *opportunity*. It's a springboard, not a pool to swim in. Christian interest in the small places must be energized by something deeper than media interest. In the past generation or two, the Christian subculture has followed the broader culture's lead in minimizing or ignoring small places. If we're only interested in small places because our broader culture is, we'll lose interest as soon as it does. I've heard Christian advocates for rural ministry try to rally excitement by making it cool again. But squeezing small towns into skinny jeans and flannel isn't good enough. Trendy things (by definition) don't last. An enduring, tenacious passion for small-place ministry must be sourced from abiding realities like the character of God and the nature of the gospel. Our broader culture's current interest offers an opportunity to look afresh at the small places—but we must look with gospel vision. What will we see when we do?

DEFINING TERMS: WHAT COUNTS AS A SMALL PLACE?

I've been using the term *small places*. The title of this book is *A Big Gospel in Small Places*. So it's important to explain what I mean by that term. I certainly don't mean *small* in a geographical sense. More than 90 percent of land in the UK is natural or farmland, by some estimates rural areas cover more than 75 percent of America's land area, and rural areas cover much of the rest of the world's land area.[7] Instead, when I refer to small places, I'm using the term in a nontechnical sense to refer to countryside and communities that are relatively small in population, influence, and economic power. I'm speaking of towns many people have never heard of, like Monson and Pepperell. I'm thinking of places like Lusk, Wyoming; the Rhondda Valley of Wales; and South Royalton, Vermont.

We can think of small places and big places on a continuum, with any given settlement of human beings falling somewhere along that line based on factors such as population, cultural influence, economic power, and degree of isolation from large urban centers. All the way on the "big place" end of that spectrum are the world's forty largest cities, which account for two-thirds of the world's economic output and shape global trends in fashion, education, entertainment, sports, and much else besides.[8] Somewhere in the middle are the suburbs and exurbs that surround these great cities. On the "small place" end of the spectrum are towns like my hometown Monson and even smaller communities, such as the 429 Maine townships that don't have any local municipal government or even a normal name—places like T3 R4 WELS or T5 ND BPP. The unorganized areas of Maine account for more than one half of its land area but contain a total of only nine thousand year-round residents. They're *very* small places!

This continuum is helpful for three reasons. First, it reminds us of the many differences between various small places (what some have called "multiple ruralities"). Though I'd plot both Monson and Pepperell on the small-place end of the spectrum, their differences are significant. Equally, an isolated agricultural town in the Midwest plains will be different in character from a small college town in the Northwest or a remote African village. These differences matter for life and ministry. We'll explore their impact later in the book.

Second, as we consider the smallness or bigness of a community based on its population, economic power, and cultural influence, we find communities of large population and high density that are nonetheless quite limited in their economic power and cultural influence. A friend lives in an economically depressed region of Manchester, England, an area that has attracted many immigrants. Though Manchester is the third-largest metropolitan area in the United Kingdom, this part of the city is relatively small in economic power and cultural influence. It may fall somewhere closer to the small-place end of the spectrum than we'd initially think. Conversely, some places small in population nonetheless have an outsized cultural influence. In the United States, two of the eight Ivy League universities are in small towns: Dartmouth in Hanover, New Hampshire (population 12,000), and Cornell in Ithaca, New York, (population 30,000). My wife graduated from the University of St. Andrews in Scotland, located in a small, picturesque town of seventeen thousand. Both the university and the golf course (which regularly hosts the British Open) have a global influence. There are certainly elements of bigness in these places.

Because there's a very sizable overlap between small places (as I'm defining them) and small towns and rural areas, I'll often use those terms nearly synonymously in this book. That's because almost all small towns and rural areas qualify as small places, while relatively few cities do. But my repeated use of the term *small places* will be both a reminder that some small towns are *larger* (in influence and economic power) than might first appear and an invitation for those in poor, uninfluential parts of the city to see the elements of *smallness* in their places.

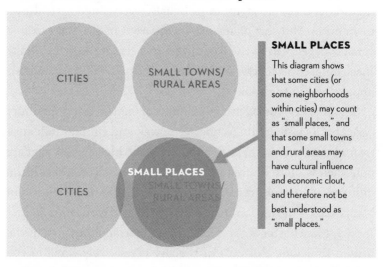

SMALL PLACES

This diagram shows that some cities (or some neighborhoods within cities) may count as "small places," and that some small towns and rural areas may have cultural influence and economic clout, and therefore not be best understood as "small places."

Third, the continuum also helps us see that any given place can contain mixed elements of rurality and urbanity—it may not be all one or the other. The current emphasis in the field of geography "resists an urban-rural binary," seeing more of a range of "urbanness" and "rurality."[9] If you think about it for a moment, you can see why. There's an arbitrariness involved in any statistical definition of *metropolitan area, urban, rural,* or *small town.* Is the definition based on population? If so, just how big must a particular cluster of people be in order to qualify as a small town or as urban? The same arbitrariness is involved when using other criteria. It turns out that demographers and government agencies use different definitions. A United Nations report on world urbanization acknowledges that "there is no common global definition of what constitutes an urban settlement" and that the definition "varies widely across countries."[10] These varying definitions lead in turn to varying definitions of *rural* because demographers usually define *rural* negatively, as "whatever is not urban." Even within the United States alone more than two dozen definitions of *rural* are used by federal agencies! Defining what constitutes a small town is equally arbitrary.[11]

But neither the arbitrariness of statistical definitions nor the sheer number of available definitions means we should stop using them. If we want to measure urban and rural populations and realities (and we should), then we have to define the terms somehow. The arbitrariness of the definitions does suggest, however, that perhaps they shouldn't be our only way of evaluating the nature of a place. A thick description that takes into account appearance, feel, and rhythm of life also matters. Pamela Riney-Kehrberg, a scholar of rural America, notes that "the issue of how a place feels guides people's perceptions of the difference between rural and urban as much as any other factor."[12]

Of course it does. Most people develop their impressions of a place by spending time in it, not by researching what the US Census Bureau says about it. Brad Roth, a pastor in Moundridge, Kansas, suggests in his book *God's Country* that "rural identity has more to do with how rural people experience the world."[13] We could say that *rural* and *urban* are quantitative (numbers, densities) and qualitative (perspectives, ways of life).

My town of Pepperell is an example of a place that's not neatly definable. Its population of twelve thousand and its proximity to Nashua, New Hampshire, and Boston disqualify it as rural or small town according to some definitions. However, few who visit Pepperell would call it a city or even a suburb. It looks, feels, and behaves like a small, New England town. There's a distinct downtown area, a white-steepled church, and a local diner. We have community rituals, including our outdoor summer concerts at the bandstand and our New England-style town meetings (which get contentious at times). We lack the accoutrements of a city or suburb: no mall, no cinema, no big museums or cultural centers, no Starbucks, not even a high school (we regionalized years ago). While Pepperell is certainly not as far along the continuum toward *small place* as Monson, it's relatively small and maintains a strong degree of rural, small-town character. The Metropolitan Area Planning Council classifies Pepperell as a "country suburb."[14] The *country* part may explain why I see a tractor drive past my house early some mornings.

I think most of us will be able to intuitively grasp whether a particular community falls more on the small place or big place end of the continuum. In this book I'll refer to various statistics and numerous studies of urban and rural areas. The relevance of these statistics to the place where you live will depend on where your community falls on the continuum. As I've pointed out, demographers define *urban* and *rural* variously, and I won't note their particular criteria every time I quote a survey or statistic. That would be distracting and unnecessary. The picture I'm painting and the case I'm making will hold true regardless.

The bottom line is that no matter which definitions we choose, there are billions of people living in small places around the world today—and *that* matters a lot. Those billions need Jesus and won't hear of him unless someone goes to them with the gospel (Romans 10:14-15). I've heard people mention the low percentage of small-town/rural dwellers in order to justify a prioritization of urban ministry. But consider that 16.4 percent of the world's population are atheists, agnostics, and religiously unaffiliated.[15] We all know it's urgently important to reach them, even though they constitute a relatively low percentage of the overall population. Percentages aside, the numbers add up to many souls. As Donnie Griggs reminds us, the total population of American small towns alone is about thirty-three million people, which is more than the populations of Morocco, Afghanistan, Venezuela, Peru, Malaysia, Saudi Arabia, Uzbekistan, Nepal, Mozambique, Ghana, North Korea, Yemen, Australia, Madagascar, Cameroon, Angola, Syria, Romania, Sri Lanka, Cote d'Ivoire, Niger, Chile, Burkina Faso, Malawi, the Netherlands, Kazakhstan—you get the picture. (The list continues with more than a hundred other countries.)[16]

CONSIDERING PLACE

We're building a theological vision for small-place ministry centered on the gospel, and we'll begin by thinking about *place*. A helpful way to deepen our understanding of small places is to increase our awareness of the often flawed attitudes of our broader culture toward them. Understanding our culture's misperceptions will help ensure that our own instincts and actions don't simply follow its lead but are informed by the Bible and sound theology. In chapters two and three, we'll discover that small places are both better—and worse—than we think.

2

Why Small Places Are Better Than We Think

I n *The Lost Continent*, writer Bill Bryson recounts his travels through thirty-eight states, over 13,978 miles, on a quest to discover the quintessential American small town he remembered from the books and movies of his youth. He was searching for a town where "Bing Crosby would be the priest" and "Jimmy Stewart the mayor." In Bryson's view, "It was inconceivable that a nation so firmly attached to small-town ideals, so dedicated in its fantasies to small-town notions, could not have somewhere built one perfect place."[1] Sadly, Bryson was disappointed in his quest. Eventually, he realized he'd need to construct his own perfect town piecemeal from the places he had visited: a Main Street here, a courthouse and hotel and fire station there. So he called his imaginary, utopic community Amalgam.

Bryson's Amalgam is a good reminder that the idyllic American town is fantasy, not reality. The more closely we examine that white picket fence, the more peeling paint we see. And this is true the world over. Rural communities, no less than the great cities, have deep shortcomings, struggles, and sins. Small places are often far worse than we realize. Many social indicators point to more desperate conditions in rural areas than in urban centers. That's why the *Wall Street Journal* has called rural America the "new inner city."[2]

However, small places are also *better* than we believe they are. And that matters a lot for ministry because we can't serve what we don't see. I have a quiet and unassuming friend who is easy to overlook in a crowd—and when I first met him, I was tempted to do just that. But as I've come to know him better over the years, I've delighted in his humor, intelligence, and wisdom, and I've also begun to see some of his shortcomings and insecurities. I love him and want to serve him however I can. When we truly see people and places, we're motivated to minister to them. That means it's really important to be shown what we're failing to see. In at least three ways, small places are often marginalized and misunderstood.

SMALL PLACES ARE OFTEN FORGOTTEN

In the year 2007 an event of great significance occurred. I'm not referring to the introduction of the first iPhone, the release of the final Harry Potter book, or the launch of the Spice Girls' reunion tour (though each of these events was, of course, highly significant in its own right). It was the year that, for the first time in human history, more people lived in cities than in rural areas.[3] The massive scale of worldwide relocation to cities is breathtaking. In 1950, about 30 percent of the world's population lived in urban areas and 70 percent in rural settlements. By 2050, just one hundred years later, that ratio will have nearly reversed.

The numbers are even more dramatic in the United States. At the time of the first American census in 1790 nearly 95 percent of the population was rural. By 2016 only about 14 percent of the US population was rural.[4] This population shift was accompanied by a massive departure from agriculture as new technologies and techniques reduced the number of farmers required to feed city dwellers.[5] Historian Richard Hofstadter famously noted that "the United States was born in the country and moved to the city."[6]

What happens when a dominant population (in this case rural residents, many of them farmers) is so rapidly reduced to minority status? There's often a deep sense of loss among those who remain. The new dominant population (in this case urban and suburban residents) sometimes overlooks rural areas altogether. When it does remember the small places, it sometimes despises and uses them.

Some have argued that rural areas are *not* forgotten, pointing to rural bias in the allocation of resources and disproportionate rural influence in the structure of the American political system.[7] But although rural America may be proportionally well-represented, the steep decline of rural populations nonetheless leads to decreasing influence nationwide. In December 2012, Agriculture Secretary Tom Vilsack spoke to a farm group in Washington, DC, warning of the increasing irrelevance of rural America in a rapidly urbanizing nation. "Unless we respond and react, the capacity of rural America and its power and its reach will continue to decline."[8] A 2013 *USA Today* article noted the difficulties that national lawmakers from rural areas face in passing legislation to aid their own communities because they're so significantly outnumbered by politicians who represent urban areas. In the same article, the state demographer of South Dakota noted, "Our rural people are not that significant. We don't have the votes. We don't have the voice." Vilsack himself has often spoken of rural America as "invisible" and "forgotten." Wendell Berry's fictional character Jayber Crow, the bachelor barber of tiny Port William, Kentucky, asks, "How many . . . invisible, nameless, powerless little places are there in this world? All the world, as a matter of fact, is a mosaic of little places invisible to the powers that be."[9]

Forgetting small places plays out in many ways. The expansion of automobile travel and America's interstate system in the twentieth century created "off-ramp towns," leading to the loss of thousands of highly diverse small settlements.[10] Even if they manage to survive, communities in the country often lack resources. Of the nineteen million Americans who don't have access to broadband internet, three-quarters live in rural areas.[11] My parents in rural Maine have found it difficult to secure urgently needed in-home health care. After Hurricane Michael ripped through Florida in October 2018, the *Washington Post* ran an article headlined "A Week After Hurricane Michael, Rural Residents Feel Stranded." One resident of tiny Alford, Florida (population 400), was quoted as saying, "You think the government would have come out to help us country folk. But we are still struggling."[12]

Many rural residents feel overlooked and invisible. The title of Robert Wuthnow's 2018 book *The Left Behind* aptly sums up their feelings. No matter how you interpret the rise of Donald Trump, it seems clear that his support from rural voters in 2016 was due largely to their sense of being forgotten. Their desire to be remembered was so powerful that they gave their votes to a fabulously wealthy urbanite who promised to give them a voice. Their voice was heard in the results of the election, but that may be the short-term exception that proves the long-term rule.

Evangelicals have participated in this forgetting too. A major shift in ministry priorities has been underway for some time. A 2016 *Washington Post* article observed that "As major ministries, conferences, book publishing, and church planting became centers of evangelical activity in urban and suburban areas in recent decades, evangelical leadership and priorities shifted away from small-town America."[13] We should all celebrate the gospel gains achieved through the urban initiatives of the past thirty years. But it's clearly the case that in the move toward urban centers the small places have been eclipsed. The city has a cool factor that the countryside simply cannot rival. A 2016 *Daily Beast* article quoted one observer as saying, "coming to New York [City] becomes the coolest thing in the world for pastors: You're getting the very best to come."[14] The well-known pastors, authors, movement leaders, and conference speakers live and minister in urban or suburban areas, and are usually not in touch with the unique needs of the rural places.

In an important 2016 *Christianity Today* article, "I Overlooked the Rural Poor—Then Trump Came Along," Tish Harrison Warren confessed her own deafness to "the suffering and frustration of impoverished whites" in the "vast open reaches of the country," admitting that "for many, rural communities and small towns are faceless places we road-trip through on our way to somewhere else."[15] Warren wondered whether "in our commitment to the city and snobbery about quality coffee," urban evangelicals "have forgotten the least of these outside the city limits." With striking candor, she confessed a conviction of sin for her ignorance of the small places.

SMALL PLACES ARE OFTEN DESPISED

For thousands of years sophisticated city dwellers have looked down on those who live in the country. Some urbanites in the Roman Empire considered rustics "clumsy, brutish, ignorant, uncivilized."[16] In fact, the Bible itself records evidence of an ancient disdain for small places. In the first chapter of John's Gospel, Nathanael asks, "Can anything good come out of Nazareth?" Nazareth was an insignificant village of only two hundred to four hundred inhabitants.[17] But perhaps something more is at play. We learn later in the Gospel that Nathanael's home village was Cana, nine miles north of Nazareth, more prosperous and considerably larger (excavations show it had about one thousand people). New Testament scholar Richard Bauckham suggests the possibility that

"Nathanael's comment expresses the disdain of a prosperous community for its smaller and poorer neighbor."[18]

At a fundraiser in San Francisco during the 2008 presidential primary campaign, candidate Barack Obama famously sparked controversy with his comments regarding small towns in Pennsylvania and the Midwest that had lost jobs and felt politically neglected: "So it's not surprising then that they get bitter, they cling to guns or religion or antipathy to people who aren't like them or anti-immigrant sentiment or anti-trade sentiment as a way to explain their frustrations."[19] Regardless of the truth (or not) of this comment, some perceived it as an example of what, in a widely read 2016 *Vox* article, the essayist Emmett Rensin termed the "smug style in American liberalism"—the belief that those not part of the liberal consensus aren't just wrong in their opinions but are fundamentally ignorant and deluded.[20] According to Rensin, the smug style is a "posture of reaction and disrespect" and a "condescending, defensive sneer." Regardless of one's politics (Rensin himself is left-leaning), there's clearly some truth here. Wuthnow identifies our culture's stereotypes of those who live in small places: "Small towns are places where village idiots reside, country bumpkins gather, and rednecks tell bigoted jokes."[21]

Of course, those in small places may bring such attitudes upon themselves, and many rural Americans despise city dwellers as much as they are despised by them. The federal government is often vilified by rural people as an out-of-touch and interfering urban enemy.[22] Conservative media outlets stoke and profit from rural rage. This mutual suspicion and animosity is evidence of a growing urban-rural divide, one it seems fewer and fewer people are attempting to bridge in order to genuinely understand one another.

Robert Wuthnow is one who is trying hard to understand. A self-described member of the "liberal elite," he's spent a decade interviewing small-town and rural Americans in order to understand them. In a 2018 interview Wuthnow admitted,

> Part of me wants to take some of these [rural] people, shake them up, and tell them to 'move on.' . . . But another part of me says it's important to understand where they're coming from and not simply dismiss them as disconnected or out of touch with reality.[23]

As I've invested in my own small community, building relationships and participating in the civic life of the town, I've been deeply impressed with the intelligence and creativity of my fellow townspeople. They have genuine concerns, good ideas, and a willingness to invest many volunteer hours to improve our local community.

Rural residents weren't always despised. Early in American history they were lauded and esteemed. Thomas Jefferson famously spoke of farmers as especially virtuous and as "the chosen people of God."[24] If anyone was suspect, it was city dwellers.[25] In fact, Jefferson believed the secret to a lasting, virtuous nation was to remain mainly agricultural, with empty lands, rather than crowding into cities.[26] As America became increasingly industrialized and urban, however, attitudes shifted dramatically. In 1924 journalist H. L. Mencken (never one to mince words) wrote, "Let the farmer, so far as I am concerned, be damned forever. To Hell with him, and bad luck to him. He is a tedious fraud and ignoramus, a cheap rogue and hypocrite."[27]

Sadly, evangelicals have sometimes despised small places. Michael Kruger identifies a mindset he calls "the arrogance of the urban," which privileges city ministry and can often lead to disdaining or caricaturing the suburbs and rural places.[28] Tim Keller rightly notes "the condescending attitudes many have toward small towns and small churches."[29] Strangely, American evangelicals grasp the importance of sending skilled workers to small places overseas but often feel differently about those who go to small places in their own country, as though they're squandering their talent and education. A *Time* magazine article noted the warning one professor gave to a gifted seminary student considering a call to rural ministry: "Don't go. You're too creative for that."[30] Author Jared Wilson reports that when he moved to a small church in a tiny Vermont town, he was warned about the potential consequences to his career.[31] One urban ministry book employs a demeaning tone: "In order to win people to Christ and plant churches, Paul didn't go to a haystack in the countryside."[32]

I understand this despising of small places because I shared it for a good portion of my adult life. But to the extent evangelicals despise the small places, we will fail them. We cannot serve what we despise. The development of a theological vision for rural and small-town ministry will include recovering respect for these places and their people—an affirmation of Francis Schaeffer's claim that there are no little people and no little places.[33] After all, it was under a haystack in a Massachusetts meadow in 1806 that a prayer meeting of five college students changed the world by launching the American Protestant missions movement. The "Haystack Prayer Meeting" led to the formation of America's first foreign mission society, which sent out well more than a thousand missionaries, most of them from small New England towns, over the next several decades.

SMALL PLACES ARE OFTEN USED

Small places lack population and influence. Because residents are scattered over the countryside, it's more difficult to rally them for political causes. Consequently, small places are more likely to be taken advantage of by larger metropolitan areas than vice versa even though the small places include the agricultural heartland that continues to feed urbanites.

There's another way small places are disadvantaged in relationship to big places: many of the young people who are loved, cared for, invested in, and educated in the small places eventually move to universities and cities, never to return. A 2017 *Wall Street Journal* article noted, "As more young people decide to pursue four-year degrees, college towns are siphoning students out of the rural heart of the Farm Belt and sending them, degrees in hand, not back to Oskaloosa but to the nation's urban centers."[34] The article reported that in 2014, rural Mahaska County sent 170 people to Johnson County, home of the University of Iowa. Johnson County, in turn, sent only twenty people back. This disparity in population flow between rural counties and the state universities is common across the country. Small-town exporting of talented kids has led to urban renaissances in big cities while creating what sociologists Patrick Carr and Maria Kefalas refer to as an "unstoppable downward cycle" in many small towns.[35] Young people leave, school enrollments decline, resources diminish, poverty and social isolation increases—and therefore (unsurprisingly) young people don't want to come back.

Evangelicals have, in our own way, participated in using small places. Seminary graduates minister there in order to prepare for what they really want to do: be a lead pastor in a bigger church in a bigger place. They're encouraged in this by those who advise them to gain experience in a small place before moving to a bigger one. A friend told me he remembers someone referring to his small church as a "starter church." Eugene Peterson, writing of his childhood church experience growing up in small-town Montana, notes that pastors never stayed for more than two to three years. And Wendell Berry offers the heartbreaking testimony that in fifty years in his rural community, "many student ministers have been 'called' to serve in its churches, but not one has ever been 'called' to stay." Instead, the small, rural communities have paid for the training of ministers who invariably go off to the big cities.[36]

I've seen this happen. My father pastored the small church in my hometown for more than thirty years. But the other church in town, after losing their much-loved pastor, saw a succession of seminary students pass through, staying until they graduated and a bigger church in a bigger place called them away.

A GOOD LIFE IN SMALL PLACES

Small places are frequently forgotten, despised, and used by our largely urban culture, and it's all too easy for Christians to go along with it. But I can testify from personal experience that life in small towns and rural areas is more fulfilling and rewarding than many imagine.

Not long ago, friends from Denver came to visit our family. After sharing a meal in our backyard, we drove a mile to a field on the edge of an old orchard. We strolled across the field and down through a forest until we came to a secluded pond. Our kids waded, swam, and fished as we talked on the bank. Afterward, we returned to our house and roasted marshmallows in our backyard. As my wife and I reflected on the evening, we felt grateful to the Creator God for designing our part of the world and placing us in it.

I frequently feel this way as I marvel at the abundant natural beauty all around us. We can put our canoe on the roof of our car and in less than ten minutes be at the Nashua River, where we see herons and swans as we paddle. There's a horse farm several hundred yards from our house, and we frequently watch horses trotting in the field across the road. These aren't sentimentalized descriptions; they're the realities we enjoy every day, the gifts of a good Creator. Anyone with eyes to see can immediately appreciate these and other gifts of small places. Evidently, many people do: though there's much migration away from rural areas in America, the small places that have bucked that trend and experienced growth are those nearer to urban areas or with natural amenities such as a mild climate, varied topography, and proximity to bodies of water.[37] Writer Julianne Couch summarizes research indicating why some people move from cities to the countryside, and the reasons include factors such as a slower pace of life, less congestion, lower cost of living, and the beauty of the natural environment.[38]

While many can immediately value the visible, tangible aspects of small-town and rural life, some of the sweetest pleasures and most surprising possibilities are deeper and more hidden. They come only through time, relationships, and a change in perspective. Small towns and rural places, like Mary Poppins's magical carpet bag, are bigger on the inside than on the outside. When you're part of a small town, when you learn its history and meet its people and experience its life, it feels bigger. Not only do you see that the brokenness is greater than cultural stereotypes suggest, but you also realize that the possibilities are more exciting than outsiders see.

This was recently brought home to me as I read a piece written about my hometown by my brother, an academic historian. He described the varied ways Monson has engaged with the wider world throughout its nearly two-hundred-year history. In the 1800s, when slate was a valued roofing material, Monson's economy boomed. A high-quality vein of slate was discovered running through town, and Swedes and Finns immigrated to Monson to dig it from the ground. They brought with them cultural traditions that continue to shape the town today: the Finnish Farmers Club dance hall sits on the edge of town, the restored Swedish Lutheran church is one of its architectural jewels, and Swedish surnames are still common. Monson slate was used on the roof of St. Patrick's Cathedral in New York City and later as the grave markers for John F. Kennedy and Jackie Kennedy Onassis. Eventually though, as cheaper roofing materials became available, the demand for slate decreased and Monson had to reinvent itself again.

The story of slate and how it has shaped my hometown is just one thread in a rich tapestry that includes Civil War letters written from Monson, the Appalachian Trail and the ecological history of the area, and the surprisingly rich artistic tradition of Monson, which includes such notables as the twentieth-century pioneering female photographer Berenice Abbott and the critically acclaimed landscape painter Alan Bray.

And the story continues. Monson is currently experiencing an unexpected chapter in its history as a philanthropic organization pours millions of dollars into remaking much of it into an artist's colony.[39] Will this radical experiment work? Will artists come to Monson? Will there be a place for locals in the newly remade Monson economy? The town is hopeful, but no one knows.

I was deeply moved as I read about Monson and realized how little I had seen or appreciated what was all around me. There was brokenness and folly and tragedy, ingenuity, humor, achievement, tenacity, and triumph. It unfolded over many generations in a tiny place, and I was mostly oblivious while I lived there. I just wanted to get away. A biographical account of the landscape artist and Monson native Alan Bray describes him as "a close, careful, and astute observer" who "frequently finds the subjects of his paintings in events and processes that elude an eye less keen."[40] That's a good description of what can make life in a small place so rich. In her spiritual geography *Dakota*, Kathleen Norris described her countercultural choice to move from New York City to a small town in South Dakota, to "live in what the rest of the world considers a barren waste." "I had to stay in place, like a scarecrow in a field, and hope for the brains to see its beauty."[41] Unfortunately, while I was living in Monson I didn't see nearly as much of the beauty of my place as I might have.

Between 2012 and 2017, James and Deborah Fallows flew their single-engine plane on multiple trips across America, visiting dozens of overlooked small towns and cities. They stayed for a couple of weeks at a time, seeking to understand how these places had responded to adversities such as crop failure or job loss. The Fallowses present a surprisingly optimistic account of life in small places; it turns out that many have found creative ways to rebound from job loss and economic difficulties and to promote healthy economies, greener lifestyles, and vibrant communities. Though the Fallowses see national politics as largely broken and ineffective, they find lots of "local resilience and adaptability" in smaller places.[42] The same is true for small towns in Europe; while their struggles are real, some have found ways to adapt and flourish through tourism, renewable energy initiatives, and the welcoming of immigrants.[43] When journalists and academics take a closer look at small places, of course they see problems—but not *just* problems. They also witness strengths and successes. When Julianne Couch visited nine communities in five Midwestern states, she saw their beauty and possibility, noting that it may even be the case that it's becoming cool among younger generations to live in rural America.[44]

For all the very real problems small places experience (I'll note some in chapter three), many people genuinely appreciate living in them. A friend recently catalogued the challenges facing his tiny rural community in the American West but concluded with an appreciation of his place: "Neighbors help neighbors. They are very generous and eager to help meet needs. They work hard and are very self-sufficient and resourceful. I love where we live even with all of its struggles." I hear this from many of my friends. Surveys have shown that people in rural places tend to be happier with where they live than their city counterparts.[45] More than that, several polls and academic studies have demonstrated that people in small places around the world tend to be happier *overall* than urban residents.[46] As reported in the *Washington Post*, re-searchers found "a striking association between population density—the concentration of people in a given area—and happiness." Based on the study, the *Post* concluded that "The farther away from cities people live, the happier they tend to be."[47] Perhaps small places really are better than we think.

A DEEPER REASON TO VALUE SMALL PLACES

There are many common grace reasons for the goodness of small places—reasons that can be seen and appreciated by anyone who cares about them and stays in them long enough to look. But there's a deeper reason why small places are better than we think. It has more to do with special grace than common grace, salvation than creation, God than human beings. It's that *God* sees them as better, more valuable, and more promising than we do. He has plans established from before time to save people who live in them. He delights to lavish his grace on them through his body, the church, making these tiny towns better for all who live in them.

Small places are valuable not just for whatever *intrinsic* value they may possess but for the value God *assigns* them. Small places are better than we think because God himself treasures them. As Brad Roth says, "The rural church represents God's commitment to be with all people, everywhere, through the church, which is Christ's [body]."[48] God often chooses weak and unimpressive things in order to make known his own great power. The gospel itself proclaims that God prizes the weak; God has a penchant for showing love to those who seem least worthy of it and least likely to influence others with it. God thinks more highly of small places than we do.

A friend once told me a story from his early years of ministry in a remote location. One day he took the Communion elements to the home of an elderly man who couldn't make it to church because of his poor health. Arriving at the house, my friend discovered that the man had soiled himself and had no one to help him. So my friend led him into the bathroom and helped him to change and wash. Then they shared the bread and wine of

Communion. With tears in his eyes, my friend told me, "It just felt so right."

Of course it did. What we celebrate at the Communion table is God's willingness to help us all in our profound weakness, cleansing our filth and forgiving our sin. Communion isn't for somebodies; it's for nobodies. Or perhaps Communion is a reminder of the surprising grace by which God counts us, in Christ, as somebodies, now known and loved by him.

Imagine looking out the window of a plane flying late at night over the heartland of America. You won't see the beautiful, brilliant light clusters of Los Angeles or Miami or New York City. You'll see only darkness and perhaps the occasional tiny glimmer of light. But far down there in the darkness are eternal souls, each known and treasured by God, infinitely valuable to him. When we look at small places, we may see insignificance—but God sees tremendous value. We may see loss, but he sees promise. We may see darkness, but he sees the hope of a new day.

3

Why Small Places
Are Worse Than We Think

THERE'S A FUNNY THING about popular views of small places. On the one hand, they're frequently despised. But, ironically, they're also idealized. This idealization is an ancient tradition, evident, for instance, in a stream of Roman poetry that exalted the agricultural life, creating a kind of "literary utopia in which the negative aspects of life [were] relegated to the city."[1] In this poetic vision, the countryside was a place of stability and family relationships. The farmer was a virtuous, industrious man. His wife helped by gathering firewood, milking the flock, and weaving. It seems the Roman poets were writing the original American country song about a hard-workin', honest, simple family man! Tim McGraw's "Where the Green Grass Grows" is a typical example of the genre—McGraw sings about the pleasures of seeing his corn growing in rows, tucking up in bed beside his wife, and raising his children in the God-blessed countryside.

Some have pointed out the many commonalities between Roman poetry and American country music.[2] But despite the similarities, there's an important difference between the Roman poets and modern country singers: namely, their personal experience of the countryside. The Roman poets tended to be educated, elite, and quite wealthy. Few had direct experience of the "happy farmers" they described; if they visited the countryside at all, their experience was a privileged one.[3] Many country singers, on the other hand, come from the places they sing about. Of course, there's often a massive disparity between the simple, frugal lives of those described in country songs and the *current* incomes and cosmopolitan lifestyles of the stars who sing the songs. But often the countryside is where the stars began and where they maintain ongoing connections.

That difference between the Roman poets and country music stars suggests an important distinction: Small places are idealized both *from the inside* and *from the outside*. Country music represents idealizing from the inside. It functions as a means of bolstering and reassuring those in small places by pushing back against urban privilege, dominance, and disdain. (The city is often vilified, along with its pompous, unfriendly, BMW-driving inhabitants.) Of course, idealizing can be a good thing, reinforcing a healthy pride in place. But it can also strengthen (and stem from) an unhealthy resistance to outside influence and help. In his memoir *Hillbilly Elegy*, J. D. Vance describes the stubborn resistance of many in Appalachian America to national media exposés of pressing regional poverty and public health problems: "This is none of your damn business." Vance cites a study showing that Appalachian teens "learn from an early age to deal with uncomfortable truths by avoiding them, or by pretending better truths exist."[4] Idealizing from the inside can be a means of avoiding uncomfortable truths and maintaining the myth that all is well. In her brutally honest essay "Gatsby on the Plains," Kathleen Norris identifies the insularity and mediocrity of small Dakota places that "idealize their isolation," fragile communities that need "to

see [themselves] as idyllic in contrast to the bad world outside."[5]
When I was growing up in rural Maine, we even had pejorative
names for those who lived outside our region. Those putdowns
helped us reinforce the myth of our own superiority.

There's also idealizing from the outside. Robert Wuthnow summarizes the perceptions of some residents of large metropolitan
areas regarding small places: "Wouldn't it be nice to live like
people used to when nobody locked their doors, the air was fresh,
morals were pure, and life was uncomplicated."[6] This is the May-
berry of Andy Griffith and the small-town USA of Norman
Rockwell, an American tradition that has been around for a long
time. In 1802 a Maine woman named Eliza Southgate wrote to
her friend: "Our novelists have worn the pleasures of rural life
threadbare."[7] Often such idyllic portrayals stem from ignorance.
As Victor Hanson notes, the growth of urban culture corresponds
to a growth in its romanticization of "the rarely visited countryside."[8] It turns out there's a connection between despising and
idealizing small places: neither attends very closely to actual
small places. Rural demographer Calvin Beale wrote, "The countryside was a time machine in which urbanites could see the living
past, and feel nostalgic or superior, as the sight inclined them."[9]

Evangelicals have participated in this idealization. Some time
ago I read an urban church-planting book that referred to the
"peaceful environment of small-town America," naively obscuring
the complex realities and deep brokenness of many small places.
Another resource spoke of idyllic towns where one could escape
the sinfulness and complexities of the city. It's all too easy to buy
into these stereotypes of simple, uncomplicated rural life. As
Patrick Carr and Maria Kefalas write, "The greatest myth of small-
town life is that nothing bad ever happens there."[10]

In my years of small-town ministry, I've repeatedly discovered
just how wrong that myth is. I've discipled a sex offender and
heard the heart-wrenching story of his small-town childhood. I've

led the funerals of young men who died in tragic accidents. I've witnessed lots of sin and despair. I will never forget a woman, "Mary," a single mother who had suffered years of physical abuse and consequently struggled with depression, suicidal desires, drug abuse, poverty, and unhealthy relationships with men. These issues sometimes left her unable to care for her son for long periods of time. Members of our small church became foster parents in order to fill the void; others offered Mary practical and emotional support; and we all regularly agonized over how to support a woman who was ricocheting from one destructive behavior to the next. Should she give up custody of her son because of her addiction? What if she never got him back? How could we possibly help her break free from her seemingly impossible situation?

Believing the myth of idyllic small-town life isn't just naive— it's dangerous. Much of the energy, vision, and resources of the evangelical church is currently focused on cities and suburbs, and there will be no equivalent impulse to mobilize Christian workers for the small places if we assume they're doing just fine. Why pour out your life for what's already near perfect? We will not fruitfully serve what we idealize. A theological vision for ministry to small places must recognize the deep sinfulness, brokenness, and complexity of people everywhere, in places big and small. Small towns and rural areas throughout the world face severe problems. Many are clinging to survival. In the words of Wendell Berry's Jayber Crow, a small town "in this age of the world is like a man on an icy slope, working hard to stay in place and yet slowly sliding downhill."[11]

A LANDSCAPE OF LOSS

If you're ever driving north on Route 15 through Monson, Maine, (I'll admit that's not very likely) and look up the hill to your right as you leave town, you'll see a health center with medical and dental offices. You won't know it by looking at the building, but it contains a story of loss and hope. I attended elementary school in that building for five years and vividly recall the giant head of a moose mounted on the wall, the friendly lunch ladies, and their sometimes-inedible creations. (We learned to hide uneaten food in our empty milk cartons.) Many generations of Monson students have attended the town's primary school, going all the way back to its founding in 1847. But in 2009, that run came to an end. The Monson Elementary School was closed that year due to a dwindling student population and lack of resources. Since then, Monson kids have been bused to a regional elementary school thirty minutes away.

It's a story that has played out across the country. The ultimate gut punch for a small community is when it can't even afford to educate its own children—or doesn't even have children to educate.[12] At least Monson parents can still send their kids to a decent school a half hour away; in many rural communities there simply are no good schools available. A friend who ministers in a poor, rural county in the American South told me the math proficiency for his county in a recent year was 8 percent. Kids graduated from the local high school without ever having been taught by a certified math teacher. Their high school building was a previously condemned elementary school. (The former high school had flooded a couple of years before.) His daughter was in an honors class in which the teacher would turn off the lights in three out of five class periods, loop YouTube videos, and let the kids sleep.

In Monson's case, the school's closing was related to another bitter loss a couple of years before. Moosehead Manufacturing Company was founded by two brothers in 1947 and became the largest furniture manufacturer in Maine. Boy, were we proud of it when I was growing up. By the late 1980s, it employed 250 people, with annual sales of almost $20 million. A sizable percentage of Monson residents worked there, including multiple generations of some families. But the day came when Moosehead could no longer compete with low-priced furniture imports, and it laid off most of its employees in 2007. Although it was temporarily saved by an investment group, a couple of years later it was running a workforce of only twenty-two full-time employees. Despite numerous efforts to stay afloat, the company eventually closed, and Monson lost all those jobs.

Robert Wuthnow refers to the "unspoken sadness" he felt while visiting a depleted town in rural Kansas, and for years I've felt that sadness in Monson. One historian describes the countryside as a "landscape of loss." What exactly is lost when a tiny town can't educate its children or when the only major employer folds? Obviously, *people* are lost. They move to find work. They move to a place that doesn't require their young child to spend an hour each day on a school bus. In 2010, Monson had 686 residents; that number is projected to decrease in coming years. But it's not just people who are lost. Schools are sources of energy, community, and pride, and a school's closing is a deep wound. Similarly, Moosehead Manufacturing was more than a source of income for local residents—it was one of the ways we identified ourselves. Moosehead's closing was a blow to the town's sense of itself.

I'm aware that I've been complicit in the decline of my hometown. I left and never came back. My name is on a plaque in the town museum for doing more pull-ups than any other kid in the history of the elementary school (nineteen, if you're curious). But other than that fleeting moment of glory, I'm no longer a part of Monson's story. I'm not raising my kids there. I'm not contributing to the local economy. I follow Monson's progress (or lack thereof) from a distance and return to visit once or twice a year, but that's about it.

Happily, there's a glimmer of unexpected hope in this particular story. There's a reason the Monson Elementary School building has become a health center rather than simply moldering into decay. The philanthropic Libra Foundation recently bought, renovated, and repurposed it as part of their multimillion-dollar renewal of the town. It seems there may be a new chapter for Monson—though who knows if an elementary school will ever again be part of the story?

But most small, struggling communities will never receive the lifeline that's been thrown to Monson. In most cases, the slow decline will simply continue. One of the benefits of the post-2016 curiosity about small places is that some observers are now seeing the daunting problems of tiny communities with greater clarity.[13] It's necessary to look closely to see these struggles.

POPULATION LOSS

One basic underlying problem for small places is the loss of residents. In some communities, population loss is the result of man-made or natural disasters.[14] In others, the industrialization of agriculture has reduced the number of farmers needed and pushed out many of the smaller ones. Of course, rural populations vary over time and place. Some decades have actually seen overall rural population growth, and rural population losses are spread unevenly around the country. Rural areas whose economies focus on human and social services have lost fewer people than communities dependent on farming, mining, or manufacturing.[15] Areas with natural amenities such as warm weather, lakes, and mountains often maintain population or even grow.

But large swaths of the rural heartland (along with other small places) are losing people, especially young people.[16] Even in countries like England, where the overall population of rural areas has grown, there's a significant loss of younger people from rural areas.[17] The departure of the younger generation means nonmetropolitan counties are rapidly aging, and experiencing a significant brain drain. This makes it more difficult to find doctors, business owners, teachers, and other professionals to replace those who retire. It leads to the shuttering of schools and churches

and businesses, to declining home values, to drop-offs in attendance and participation in community groups and organizations.
And "perhaps most importantly, population decline devastates
morale and nurtures a conservatism that prevents residents from
taking the risks that might reverse their decline."[18]

Often the decisive break comes when kids venture away to
college. Studies have demonstrated that individuals with a college
education are much more likely to live in a state other than their
birth state than those without one.[19] State governments have
been creative in their attempts to bring young people back to
rural areas, offering tax cuts and credits to educated young adults.
As part of their "Come Back to Iowa, Please" initiative, Iowa
mailed two hundred thousand letters to young people, asking
them to return and settle down. But most of these initiatives
have produced only meager results. And Patrick Carr and Maria
Kefalas highlight the ironic reality that rural teachers, parents,
and leaders often participate in the demise of their own small
places by "[investing in] the young people destined to leave and
[ignoring] the ones most likely to stay or return."[20] All too often,
the decrease of rural populations leads to an increase of rural
problems for those who remain.

POVERTY AND JOB LOSS

The economic news in many rural places is bad. Poverty rates in
rural America exceed poverty rates in urban areas and have far
fewer social services available to help.[21] Children are often affected. The United States Department of Agriculture reports that
one in four children in rural America lives in poverty. Moreover,
"Rural child poverty rates are higher than for urban children of
every racial and ethnic group, and the highest poverty rates are
in the most rural places."[22] A ministry friend told me about a
parentless sixteen-year-old boyfriend and girlfriend in a West
Virginia town. They're squatting in a vacant, burned-out home,

eating school meals. Because rural poverty is scattered over physical space (unlike concentrated urban poverty) it's often relatively invisible, leading many to believe it's not the tremendous problem it actually is.[23]

A closely related problem is joblessness. The outsourcing of American manufacturing jobs overseas particularly affects rural areas, since more than one-third of rural employment depends on goods-producing industries.[24] In 2016 the Brookings Institution reported that work rates among prime-aged men were considerably lower in rural areas than in cities and suburbs.[25] Moreover, the job situation got worse for rural areas between 2000 and 2014, while simultaneously improving in cities. The Brookings report concludes that

> the past 10-15 years have strengthened the economic hand of many cities, as coming-of-age generations seek a more urban lifestyle, and as an increasingly services-focused U.S. economy concentrates in places with greater access to highly skilled labor, innovative institutions, and strong global connectivity. . . . Those same dynamics have simultaneously disadvantaged many small towns and rural areas.

It's no wonder so many residents of small communities are moving to cities.

THE RURAL DRUG EPIDEMIC

Drugs have usually been seen as an inner-city problem, and of course they are. But death rates from drug overdoses in rural parts of the United States now outpace the rate in large metropolitan areas.[26] Some drug and alcohol use may be attributable to the boredom that rural young people experience.[27] A pastor from Wyoming told me, "Teenage drinking is a huge problem fueled by a lack of other things to do." My own congregation has been affected by drug and alcohol addiction. We've sought to walk alongside those struggling with addiction while dealing with the enormous personal and family fallout their struggle always entails. A local pastor told me he sees drug deals in his church parking lot. In nearby New Hampshire, almost five hundred people died from drug overdoses in a recent year—yet largely rural New Hampshire is second to last in the nation in access to treatment programs.[28]

Much of the recent increase in drug use is due to the rise of opioids. Though the opioid epidemic affects the entire United States, it's especially severe in rural, largely white communities. Jobs in rural areas often include more manual labor and injury, which may increase prescription opioid abuse. Compounding the problem is the fact that there aren't adequate resources available for addicts in many rural areas. West Virginia has the highest overdose rate in the United States. (One West Virginia pastor describes twenty-six overdoses in a four-hour period in his small city of 48,000 people.) Professor of psychology Kevin Eames notes that in rural Appalachia, "Poverty tends to produce family dysfunction, which is passed down from generation to generation. A combination of hopelessness, emotional wounds, and physical pain make substance abuse highly likely."[29]

Before the rise of opioids, methamphetamines had a devastating effect on the countryside. In the years after 1994, meth use nearly tripled, and the Drug Enforcement Agency reported that "by 1999, there were three hundred times more meth-lab seizures in Iowa than in New York and New Jersey combined."[30] As time went on there were significant victories, and meth use declined. But in recent years it has returned with a vengeance, compounding the already massive problem of opioid addiction. In places like rural Vinton County, Ohio, the principal of a local school reports that meth is now a bigger problem than opioids.[31] Rural areas like Vinton County are particularly hard hit because of their relative lack of resources. Andy Chambers, an addiction psychiatrist and researcher, suggests that a "broken mental health care system" underlies the drug epidemic. In Vinton County, there's not a single hospital or in-patient treatment facility, and the county prosecutor reports that it's difficult to find mental health professionals who can help users in custody. A particularly heart-breaking aspect of the rural meth crisis is its effect on children. In Vinton County, the local school principal knows of sixty students directly affected (about one sixth of the student body). The school staff maintains a storage room with underwear, socks, shoes, pants, and T-shirts for children whose addicted parents neglect them.

MANY OTHER PROBLEMS

In 2017 a publication from the Centers for Disease Control reported that rural areas had higher death rates in 1999–2014 than did metropolitan areas.[32] A subsequent study in the *American Journal of Public Health* confirmed and extended this finding, showing that from 1999–2015 the only nine subpopulations with increased death rates were all white and mainly living outside large urban areas.[33] Among all middle-age adults, rural whites had the greatest increase in death rates, an increase due mostly to suicide, accidental poisoning, and liver disease as well as chronic disease deaths. These are the so-called "despair deaths," which are increasing among "working-class whites" (defined as those with a high school education or less) as they face worsening job prospects leading to addiction, dysfunction in families, and poor social support.[34] The authors of the article in the *American Journal of Public Health* suggest reasons why rural whites have greater death rates. Rural communities face the loss of skilled workers, decreased production of goods, and fewer job opportunities. Residents experience greater isolation, have less access to health care, and manifest "striking differences in health behavior and attitudes, such as higher rates of smoking, sedentary activity, and stigmatization of mental illness." I've seen close-up the discouragement and despair caused by a toxic combination of ill health and joblessness. The future looks bleak for people in such a situation.

Many more problems could be mentioned. The Population Reference Bureau indicates higher fatality rates in rural areas for infants, young adults, middle-aged adults, and victims of motor vehicle accidents. One speaker at a conference I attended several years ago noted that women in small rural areas report the highest incidence of domestic violence, yet the mean distance to the nearest resource for a rural abused woman is three times more than for a woman in urban or suburban areas.[35] Teen birth rates are consistently higher in rural areas than in cities.[36] A friend who ministers in the rural Rhondda Valley of Wales told me he was first called there years ago when he heard that the suicide rate was the highest in the United Kingdom, teenage pregnancy was the highest in the United Kingdom, and regular church attendance of any kind was less than 1 percent.

Clearly, rural areas and small towns are not the quaint, idyllic communities lauded in country songs and imagined by urbanites. Television programs featuring unshaven, gap-toothed, rough-around-the-edges but wholesome and harmless rednecks may amuse and entertain suburban and urban viewers, but they don't begin to tell the real story of hurt, loss, dysfunction, and devastation. In so many ways, the small places are a mess.

A PROBLEM UNDERNEATH THE OTHERS

J. D. Vance recounts a summer he spent working at a floor-tile distribution business near his Ohio hometown. The company employed twelve people, paying them decent wages with steady raises—enough to put them well above the poverty line. Yet surprisingly, the warehouse manager couldn't fill all the available positions with long-term employees. Vance's coworker Bob was nineteen and had a pregnant girlfriend. She was given a clerical position at the company, but unfortunately she missed a third of her workdays without any notice and was eventually fired. Bob, too was always late, regularly missed work, and took bathroom breaks that lasted up to an hour. He was eventually fired as well. When that happened, he blamed his manager and protested that he had a pregnant girlfriend.

Vance sees the incident with Bob as an example of a larger problem that runs deep in his hillbilly culture. He sees people "reacting to bad circumstances in the worst way possible," as part of "a culture that increasingly encourages social decay instead of counteracting it." Vance perceives "a lack of agency here—a feeling that you have little control over your life and a willingness to blame everyone but yourself."[37] Vance clearly believes that much of the responsibility for the problems of hillbillies is their own. "We created [the problems], and only we can fix them."

Eliza Southgate, the Maine woman writing to her friend in 1802, wrote, "We must know there is as much depravity and consequently as much discontent in the inhabitants of a country village as in the most populous city." The problems faced by people who live in small places are partly our own doing, owing to our own depravity. People are sinful wherever they live. It's important to acknowledge that small places are worse than we think not simply because of the social ills there but because of the people there. A robust doctrine of sin reminds us of that.

But it's not as simple as saying country problems are due to sin. Beneath small-place struggles is a potent mix of sin and despair, culpability and hopelessness.[38] Vance suggests that his people aren't lazy. Rather, they experience "learned helplessness," a fatalistic belief that things will always be the same and can't be changed. One friend in an economically depressed rural area describes "a heaviness of heart and spirit. A belief that things will not get better."

Recall that the *American Journal of Public Health* report found that many of the economic and social factors in rural areas contributed to higher death rates. There's an important question to ask regarding that finding: if economic and social factors are responsible, why are *whites* inordinately affected? After all, African Americans experience enormous challenges due to many decades of systemic oppression, injustice, and racism, and they live in many of those same rural areas. The authors of the report suggest that one reason for the difference may be varying expectations; because white people have different expectations of what their lives should or will be like, and because they're clearly doing less well than their parents, they experience more despair than other groups.[39] There's a mingling of hopelessness and sin undergirding the problems of rural places. Sinful people participate in a culture that increases their sense that they'll never get out or move up, no matter what they do.

SMALL PLACES ARE BETTER AND WORSE

Small places are simultaneously better and worse than we think. Those of us who have experienced God's redeeming love in Jesus Christ are uniquely equipped to grasp this paradoxical reality because we've already experienced it in our own lives. As Tim Keller reminds us, "The gospel is this: We are more sinful and flawed in ourselves than we ever dared believe, yet at the very same time we are more loved and accepted in Jesus Christ than we ever dared hope."[40] The gospel isn't God telling us we're smarter or better-looking or friendlier than we thought we were. Rather, the good news is that God declares his love and acceptance of us in Jesus Christ despite our glaring faults.

The same is true for small places. Yes, the Creator God has blessed them and made them beautiful. But more than that, the gospel shows that he treasures them even in their smallness, slowness, anonymity, and lack of high culture. At the same time, they exist in a fallen world, and fallen people live in them. We need to see rural areas and small towns as simultaneously dark and bright places. We'll see them that way only if we allow our thinking to be reframed around the gospel.

As Christians, our erroneous views of small places are a major problem because they keep us from serving these places or from serving them well. We can't love or serve what we despise or idealize. By teaching us to be simultaneously hopeful and realistic, the gospel prevents us from both despair and naiveté. That small places are better than we thought demonstrates that they're worth all the care, participation, and service we offer. That they're worse than we thought demonstrates that there are more than enough needs to warrant a lifetime of ministry.

In an interview, J. D. Vance was asked whether Barak Obama's 2008 campaign remarks about poor white voters (the remarks about clinging to guns and religion) were in fact quite similar to Vance's own views and if perhaps Obama had been right after all. Vance acknowledged that Obama had meant well and had perceived real problems. But he noted that Obama's comments lacked sympathy. This idea of sympathy is important. Joshua Rothman writes that in *Hillbilly Elegy*

> Vance is after a certain kind of sympathy: sympathy among equals that doesn't demean or condescend. Such sympathy can't be deterministic and categorical. In fact, it must be a little judgmental; it must see the people to whom it's extended as dignified individuals who retain their moral obligations. . . . [S]ympathy that fails to recognize culpability also fails to recognize potentiality. It becomes a form of giving up.[41]

This is an important insight for Christians who consider the small places. We're called to view these places with a sympathy "that doesn't demean or condescend" because we recognize residents of small places as our equals—as sinners just like us. Simultaneously, our sympathy must "be a little judgmental," must "recognize culpability"; it must seek to engage with those in small places as "dignified individuals who retain their moral obligations." Otherwise, we've just given up on them, throwing hope overboard.

God will call some of us to do more than *consider* the small places. He'll call some of us to live and minister in them. How can we minister fruitfully in these beautiful, broken places? We'll consider that question in part two.

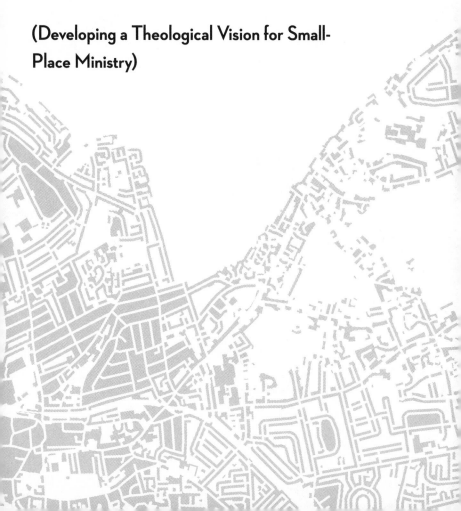

PART 2
HOW CAN WE MINISTER FRUITFULLY IN SMALL PLACES?

(Developing a Theological Vision for Small-Place Ministry)

4

The Source and Goal of Small-Place Ministry

A SHAPING GOSPEL AND A SEE-THROUGH CHURCH

I T'S 4:30 a.m. on Sunday morning, and I'm lying wide awake in bed, trying to stay still so that I don't wake my wife. I'm thinking about several people who are drifting away from Christ and the church, and I'm wondering if there's something I could be doing to help them come back. That reminds me of another sticky pastoral situation I really need to address and haven't yet, and that, in turn, calls to mind what I heard just yesterday—someone at church is angry with me.

In the midst of these swirling thoughts, I feel once again a deep yearning to be doing the work of ministry: reaching more people with the gospel and seeing greater spiritual transformation among our members. By now it's 5:30, and I know my alarm will go off soon.

While these types of doubts and anxieties seem to land on me most forcibly early on Sunday mornings, they can come anytime. If you minister in a small place and you're anything like me, you want to know how to do it better. You long to be more effective. You're passionate to see more conversions, positive change in your church culture, greater gospel influence in your town.

Maybe feelings of inadequacy aren't a problem for you. Instead, your confidence is strong and your energy is high, but you're looking for ways to become even more effective. You're eager for practical advice you can sink your teeth into, some tips you can implement, starting today. Maybe you're eager to hear best practice in rural church planting or suggestions on how to live on mission in your town.

I promise we'll get to some of these things—but not quite yet, and here's why: I believe that rural and small-town pastors and lay leaders need something more and deeper than ministry tips.

We need theological roots for what we're doing, and we need to know the end goal for why we're doing it. We desperately need a theological vision that motivates and molds our ministries. We need to see small places the way God sees them.

Why? Because all the practical tips in the world won't sustain us in the hardships of ministry or produce the *kind* of gospel ministry that will change our towns. Tips can inform our practice, but they can't transform our hearts. Tips are external add-ons to ministry, not core, inner shapers of ministry. Tips are like hubcaps for your car; theological vision is the engine and the frame. We don't simply need tips on *how* to do small-place ministry; we need to be motivated by considering *why* to do it. Offering tips without an undergirding theology is putting the cart before the horse: an arrangement that goes nowhere productive. But when practical ministry advice is deeply grounded in the gospel we embrace and is closely in touch with the larger culture we inhabit, it becomes hugely helpful.

A THEOLOGICAL VISION

The term *theological vision* comes from theologian Richard Lints and refers to a way of seeing the world that derives from the foundation of Scripture and is influenced by our approach to the use of church tradition, engagement with culture, and understanding human reason. In *The Fabric of Theology*, Lints says,

> A theological vision allows [people] to see their culture in a way different than they had ever been able to see it before. The vision gives them new eyes on the world and forces them to take a prophetic stance in each of the pieces of culture that are addressed. Those who are empowered by the theological vision do not simply stand against the mainstream impulses of the culture but take the initiative both to understand and speak to that culture from the framework of the Scriptures.[1]

Drawing on and developing Lints's concept of theological vision, Tim Keller has taught a generation of urban pastors its importance. According to Keller, theological vision is "the middle space between doctrine and practice—the space where we reflect deeply on our theology and our culture to understand how both of them can shape our ministry."[2] It's "something more practical than just doctrinal beliefs but much more theological than 'how-to steps' for carrying out a particular ministry."[3] In fact, it's "a vision for what you are going to *do* with your doctrine in a particular time and place."[4] Keller suggests that we ask the following questions in order to develop a theological vision for ministry:

- What is the gospel, and how do we bring it to bear on the hearts of people today?

- What is this culture like, and how can we both connect to it and challenge it in our communication?

- Where are we located—city, suburb, town, rural area—and how does this affect our ministry?

- To what degree and how should Christians be involved in civic life and cultural production?

- How do the various ministries in a church—word and deed, community and instruction—relate to one another?

- How innovative will our church be and how traditional?

- How will our church relate to other churches in our city and region?

- How will we make our case to the culture about the truth of Christianity?[5]

As these questions make clear, context and location matter a lot for theological vision. While the gospel is unchanging, every Christian and every church exists in a particular place, in a particular time, within a particular culture. A fruitful ministry will not *abandon* the gospel by overcontextualizing to its place and culture, nor will it *privatize* the gospel by undercontextualizing to its place and culture.[6] Put another way, it won't become syncretistic (simply blending in) or sectarian (only standing out).[7] Instead, as Keller suggests, it will appreciate and adapt, but also challenge and confront. Stephen Um and Justin Buzzard rightly note that the Bible doesn't tell us to love our place and hate God; nor does it ask us to love God and hate our place. Instead, we're called to love both God and our place, living distinctively and engaging deeply.[8]

The importance of knowledge and understanding of local culture and place was brought home to me years ago in a humorous and memorable way. Our local diner used to be called the Pepperell Spa, which always struck me as an odd name, because it was definitely not a day spa providing massages and facial treatments. It was a diner providing eggs and bacon. (I've been told that the "spa" reference may have been due to the fact that the diner once boasted a soda fountain.) One day I was speaking on the phone with a man who had lived a rough life in a tough city and had served some jail time. He was spiritually open and seeking, and we agreed to meet in person. But after I suggested that we get together at the Pepperell Spa, there was a long, awkward silence on the other end of the phone line. I've smiled to myself many times since then as I imagine him wondering why his pastor thought that enjoying a foot massage and a facial together would be of any spiritual benefit whatsoever. Local knowledge and local context matter a lot!

Keller's theological vision for ministry has grown from, and is mainly intended for, *big* places—great cities and cultural centers. It has resulted in abundant fruit as Redeemer City to City has planted hundreds of thriving churches in major world cities and as skilled and thoughtful city planters around the world have considered how the gospel alternately challenges and affirms various aspects of their urban cultures.

Because context matters greatly for theological vision, and because there are significant differences between big and small places (we've explored some in part one of this book), those who minister in small places cannot simply adopt Keller's deeply urban theological vision. That suit of clothes won't fit every minister or ministry. Instead, the challenge and opportunity for small-place ministers is to draw upon the helpful work of our city brothers and sisters in order to formulate a distinctively *small-place* theological vision. We need an understanding of how doctrinal commitments will translate into small-place ministry values, which will then shape small-place ministry practice.

Because the evangelical church has all too often despised and ignored small places, there isn't much of an evangelical theological vision for what it means to minister in them. A notable contrast is the Church of England, which has poured considerable resources into understanding and addressing the needs of the rural church in England.[9] I don't intend to formulate a comprehensive theological vision for ministry in small places in this book. Rather, I hope simply to contribute to that work and invite others to join in. The participation of many small-place pastors and lay leaders from around the world in developing such a vision is particularly important because, as we've seen, there isn't just one rural culture but many. That means a truly small-place theological vision will be formed by numerous culturally engaged, gospel-oriented, small-place Christians. My aim in this book is to prepare the way for more work to come by showing how a fruitful, small-place theological vision can flow from the gospel itself, engaging with the realities of the small places we've already observed in part one.

A SHAPING GOSPEL

Let's go right to the source of a theological vision for small-place ministry. This book is called *A Big Gospel in Small Places*. We've already given attention to small places; now we'll unpack the term *gospel*. It's important to be explicit about our understanding of the gospel because it's all too easy to read our own misunderstandings into a muddy articulation of the gospel. Some years ago, when our oldest son, Samuel, was young and often awakening us in the middle of the night, I got up extra early on Easter Sunday morning to prepare for our church's Easter sunrise service. After showering, I came back into the room to wake my wife and said cheerily, "Happy Easter—he has risen!" My sleep-deprived wife rolled over in bed and groaned, "Oh, is Samuel up already?" Perhaps our misunderstandings of the gospel proclamation aren't *that* mistaken! But if the Bible's clear articulation of the gospel doesn't shape our thinking, our thinking will fashion our own self-generated gospel, one that conforms to our own expectations. So we must ask, What is the biblical gospel?

The gospel is the good news of the salvation God has accomplished through the incarnation, death, and resurrection of Jesus Christ. In the New Testament the term *gospel* has a narrower and a broader focus.[10] The narrower focus deals with Jesus' incarnation, death, resurrection, and reign—and also with how people are saved. It's *good* news because Jesus has already accomplished salvation for us and we receive it as a gift through faith alone. In Don Carson's words, the gospel is the "good news that God is reconciling sinners to himself through the substitutionary death of Jesus."[11] Paul adopts this narrower focus in 1 Corinthians 15, when he says his gospel message is that Christ died for our sins, was buried, and then was raised on the third day, appearing to his disciples. The broader focus of the gospel deals with "the mighty dimensions of what Christ has secured," including the presence of the kingdom of God and God's renewal of the whole world through Christ.[12] It's important and helpful to recognize the gospel's broader focus so long as we don't neglect the narrower focus in doing so. This gospel of Jesus Christ is a *big* gospel in at least four ways. It's big in terms of its *importance*: it's the most urgently needed news anyone could ever hear (Romans 10:13-15). It's big in terms of its *power*: it's the power of God for salvation (Romans 1:16). It's big in terms of its *effects*: this is the broader sense of the gospel, that God is bringing his kingdom, remaking not just individual people but the entire cosmos through Jesus Christ (Matthew 24:14; Colossians 1:5). Finally, the gospel is big in terms of its *centrality*: it's the central reality of the Christian life, not just one more thing for Christians to know in addition to other things. God uses the gospel not just to save us initially (to *make* us Christians) but to transform our lives *as* Christians (Colossians 1:5-6).

This last point is an especially rich insight for Christian life and ministry. The gospel isn't just the thing that gets us in, but it's also the good news that keeps us in and progressively changes us once we're in. It's not just our gym pass; it's our personal trainer. We never move beyond the gospel to a newer, higher, more advanced message. Christian growth occurs—and Christian ministry becomes increasingly joyful, God-honoring, and effective—as we sink deeper into the gospel and align our lives and ministries more fully to it. Grasping this truth makes us lifelong learners of the gospel, just as Martin Luther, in his inimitable way, said,

> Particularly when you hear an immature and unripe saint trumpet that he knows very well that we must be saved by the grace of God, without our own works, and then pretend that this is a snap for him, well, then have no doubt that he has no idea of what he is talking about and probably will never find out. For this is not an art that can be completely learned or of which anyone could boast that he is a master. It is an art that will always have us as pupils while it remains the master.[13]

We see the central and shaping influence of the gospel in Galatians 2, where the apostle Paul reports a clash that occurred between him and the apostle Peter in Antioch. The confrontation took place because Peter had withdrawn from table fellowship with Gentiles. In his letter, Paul tells the Galatians that the conduct of Peter, Barnabas, and other Jewish Christians was not "in line with the truth of the gospel" (v. 14 NIV). It's important to notice two things in that little phrase.

First, Paul refers not simply to the gospel but to "*the truth* of the gospel*." The gospel has objective content. It is news. It announces, "Jesus has died for your sins. Jesus has risen. Jesus reigns. Your sins are forgiven as you trust in him." Moreover, the gospel's claims aren't merely truth claims—they are *true* truth claims. We know they're true because the gospel is from God himself (Galatians 1:11-12). This God-given gospel has authority over every person. To get out of step with it is to stand condemned (Galatians 2:11).

Second, Paul's phrase "*in line with* the truth of the gospel" shows that the gospel has clear implications. Like a tree, the gospel has a grain. It points us in certain directions and away from others. We either walk in line or out of line with it. In his essay "The Centrality of the Gospel," Tim Keller concludes from Galatians 2:14 that "we see that the Christian life is a process of renewing *every* dimension of our life—spiritual, psychological, corporate, social—by thinking, hoping, and living out the 'lines' or ramifications of the gospel."[14] God means for the gospel to be not merely the content of our speech but the contour of our lives. He wants our ministries and churches to increasingly take on the very shape of the gospel, embodying and expressing it. This means that our ministries must not only refer to the gospel verbally; they should also reflect the gospel holistically.

The central, shaping influence of the gospel has massive implications for life and ministry in small places. If we really believe that the gospel informs everything, shouldn't we expect it to speak into the many aspects of small-place culture, supporting some and subverting others? Shouldn't we look to the gospel in order to be shaped as small-place ministers? The gospel of Jesus Christ is the focused expression of the character of God himself (1 John 4:10). It shows us what he is like and how he relates to the world he has made. Thus it's the best possible source for developing and deepening a God-oriented theological vision for small-place ministry.

It's common to speak of Christian workers "taking the gospel" to various places. But we'll see in the following chapters that it's actually the other way around: the gospel takes *us* to places (including small ones). Discovering and delighting in the nature of God through the gospel leads us to discard worldly values we've adopted from our culture and adopt new values that send some of us to small places, shape our ministries there, and sustain us for the long haul.

A SEE-THROUGH CHURCH

If the gospel is the nourishing source of a theological vision for small-place ministry, what's the *goal*? To understand why God wants churches in small places, we must see why he wants any churches anywhere. The apostle Paul tells us in his letter to the Ephesians:

> To me, though I am the very least of all the saints, this grace was given, to preach to the Gentiles the unsearchable riches of Christ, and to bring to light for everyone what is the plan of the mystery hidden for ages in God, who created all things, so that through the church the manifold wisdom of God might now be made known to the rulers and authorities in the heavenly places. (Ephesians 3:8-10)

We can understand Paul's remarkable claim in verse 10—that through the church the manifold wisdom of God is made known to the rulers and authorities in the heavenly places—in four steps. The first is to see that God possesses "manifold wisdom" (v. 10). God notices every nuance of every reality. His wisdom is varied and vast. And it doesn't consist merely in knowing things but in *planning* them. His all-encompassing wisdom has produced an all-encompassing plan for the universe, a plan so big that it includes all time and all space (Ephesians 1:10). This infinitely wise plan is "to unite all things in [Jesus Christ]." In other words, at the last day God will publicly demonstrate that Jesus Christ is the main point of all created things. They were created "through him and for him" (Colossians 1:16). He's why they exist. Thus Jesus is the key to understanding everything else. We live in a Jesus-centric universe.

The second step is to see that God cares deeply about "making known" his manifold wisdom (Ephesians 3:10). He wants others to see and savor it. In fact, his purpose for all of history is to bring about the praise of his own glory (Ephesians 1:6, 12, 14). But he's not content to wait until the end of time for that to happen. Ephesians 3:10 says he wants his wisdom to "*now* be made known." His intended audience for this present display is the entire universe, specifically the spiritual beings, good and evil ("rulers and authorities in the heavenly places").

How will God, already in the present, display his wisdom to the universe *now*? He'll do it "through the church" (v. 10). He'll give Jesus-believing Gentiles a completely equal footing with Jews as full members of his people and partakers of his promises. Why will this make known his manifold wisdom? Because as the "rulers and authorities in the heavenly places" behold the new unity of Jew and Gentile achieved by God in Christ, they'll witness a preview of God's all-wise, all-encompassing purpose to unite *all things* in heaven and on earth in Christ (Ephesians 1:7-10). They'll see now, in the course of time, God's purpose for all time.

Finally, if the unified Jew-Gentile church is God's means of showing his wisdom to the universe already in the present, how does God intend to establish that unified Jew-Gentile church? Through the gospel. According to Paul, "the Gentiles are fellow heirs, members of the same body, and partakers of the promise in Christ Jesus *through the gospel*" (Ephesians 3:6 emphasis mine). God chose Paul to preach that gospel: "Of this gospel I was made a minister according to the gift of God's grace, which was given me by the working of his power. To me . . . this grace was given, to preach to the Gentiles the unsearchable riches of Christ" (Ephesians 3:7-8).

We can summarize like this:

THE GOSPEL	A UNIFIED JEW-GENTILE CHURCH	THE PRESENT DISPLAY OF GOD'S WISDOM	THE FUTURE PRAISE OF GOD'S GLORY

Two things here are enormously encouraging for small-place ministry. First, in God's plan there's a disproportionate relationship between the means and the ends. Paul's humble proclamation of the gospel (he's suffering in prison) and the humble presence of a church in Ephesus produce the greatest results imaginable: God's wisdom made known to the universe and God's character praised forever. No matter how small our ministry or how much suffering it entails, as we steward the grace of the gospel (Ephesians 3:2) God will manifest his wisdom and display his glory. We don't control the size of our platform or the degree of our suffering. God does. But as we remain centered on the gospel, we can be certain nothing will be wasted.

Second, when Paul says this present display of God's wisdom is accomplished "through the church" (v. 10), he isn't referring so much to what the church does as to what it *is*. The very presence of a Jew-Gentile church unified around Jesus shows God's wisdom to the universe. This means that God composes and orders his church (made up of normal people, in Ephesus or any-where else) for the purpose of showing love to his people and displaying something about himself. You might say the church is designed to be see-through. The rest of the universe is meant to look at and through the church and learn something about God.[15]

When I officiate at weddings, I sometimes charge the happy couple to pray and aspire toward a marriage that is more like a window than a wall. When we look at a wall, I tell them, our gaze stops at the wall. A wall may be a gorgeous color, beautifully deco-rated, and pleasant to look at, but at its best, it's still just a wall. The value of a window, on the other hand, is almost endless, be-cause its worth is not in itself but in what we see through it. (We usually notice windows themselves only when they're dirty or cracked; when a window is doing its job, we forget about it alto-gether.) Even an ordinary window can reveal spectacular, sur-prising things. There's nothing special about the windows in my house, but through them I've seen gorgeous birds at our feeder, green shoots and new buds in the spring, and even local teens staging outdoor Star Wars fights after dark with fake light sabers.

These images of a window and wall are my way of illustrating Ephesians 5, where Paul says that marriage "refers to" something beyond itself. In other words, marriage is meant to be the context for deep human love—and also a window to something greater. When we look through a marriage, we're meant to see the most beautiful and spectacular reality in the universe: the mutual love of Christ and his church. Marriage offers a view of the gospel itself. Good marriages are see-through. Something I've come to realize more recently is that the same is true for singleness. When Christian singles pursue God, trust God, obey God, and are satisfied in God in their singleness, they are living pictures of the ultimate satisfaction in God that all God's people will feel forever. In the eschatological kingdom, we'll all be single (Matthew 22:30). Thus Christian singles who live for God now are a foretaste and precursor of all God's people.[16] They uniquely display something of God's glory that married people don't and can't. God has arranged things so that both single and married people who live for God each uniquely display something of the glory of Christ and his gospel. Just as I need multiple windows in my house in order to see all the beauty outside (and those glowing light sabers across the street), so the church needs both single and married people in order fully to appreciate God and his good plans for us.

What if it's the same with the church itself? Ephesians 3 shows that the purpose of the church is to manifest God's glory. Can any one church or any one *kind* of church capture all of it? God used four Gospels to reveal Jesus. Might he choose to place his multifaceted glory—his power, creativity, love, patience, kindness, gentleness—on full display through many different kinds of churches in many different kinds of places? Wouldn't we expect God to show forth various aspects of his character with particular clarity through churches wealthy and poor, big and small, in big and small places, of various cultures and ethnicities and classes?

I think the answer is yes. One of the great purposes of any church, no matter what kind, is to become see-through to distinctive aspects of the character of God as revealed in the gospel. There will be some facets of God's character and God's gospel that my small church in my small town simply can't display as well as a three-thousand-member church in a great city. But the opposite will be true as well. Some precious facets of the gospel will be seen more clearly in a small church in a small place than anywhere else. Church success is usually evaluated by measuring external results, such as the number of attenders and conversions and the size of the building and budget. But what if our criteria for evaluating ministry success included "see-throughability" to God? What if we considered this question: How is our church uniquely contributing to the universe-wide display of God's character expressed in the gospel of Jesus Christ?

The nourishing *source* of small-place ministry is the gospel. The necessary *goal* of small-place ministry is the glory of God made distinctively manifest through his church in small places. Through the gospel, God creates and shapes his church in small places; through the church in small places, God adorns and displays his gospel. So the question for us is: What does this actually look like in small places? Let's find out.

5

Strategic Isn't Always What We Think

O N OCTOBER 13, 2010, a grimy, bedraggled man was hauled out of a hole in the ground and fell into the arms of his wife and son. It was a stunning moment for the millions watching on live television. Sixty-nine days earlier, he and thirty-two other Chilean miners had been trapped half a mile below ground, where they remained for the next two months as the world waited anxiously and rescuers worked frantically to free them. Finally, all thirty-three men were hoisted, one at a time, to the surface.

How much is it worth to rescue one miner and reunite him with his family? How about all thirty-three? Chilean president Sebastian Pinera estimated the cost of the rescue mission at $10-20 million, and he spoke for the Chilean people when he said, "Every peso was well spent."

Every so often, a situation like this reminds us of the immense value of every human life. In June-July 2018, when twelve Thai children and their soccer coach were trapped for two weeks in a flooded cave, no one counted the cost or questioned the use of extraordinary resources (ten thousand people took part in the rescue operation) for just a few kids. There's something valuable for us to learn from these stories.

A STRATEGIC MINISTRY

Here's an important question every person ministering in small places ought to consider: Am I making the best possible use of my life? If we're fortunate, God may grant us forty to fifty years of productive ministry for his glory. Doesn't it make sense to invest those few years in the most strategic way possible, influencing people who will influence other people? There are more eternal souls living in the densely populated cities of our world today than ever before—more than in the small places. Moreover, cities are the centers of culture and power. They contain inordinate numbers of young people, with more constantly flooding in from small towns and rural areas. This younger generation will become leaders in society, influencing countless others. Imagine you're on a sinking ship and hope to save as many people as possible. Isn't it wisest to focus your attention on ensuring the safety of the strongest swimmers, who will then save others, rather than focusing on people you know can't swim? If you want your life to count, in other words, why not pack your bags and move to the nearest city?

A good part of the emphasis on city ministry in the past generation of evangelicalism has come from the strategic desire to maximize Christian influence in the culture for the sake of spreading the gospel. Ed Stetzer summarizes it this way: "Reach the cities, reach the world; reach the cities, influence culture."[1] Tim Keller says, "As the city goes, that's how the society goes. If you win the countryside and you ignore the cities, you've lost the culture. But if you win the city and you ignore the countryside, you've won the culture."[2] According to this way of thinking, reaching the younger, urban generation—the creative class—with the gospel and influencing (or creating) culture-making institutions will shape the worldview of the broader culture and prepare the way for the gospel to advance.

There is much to commend in this view. Cities exert massive, outsized influence in education, government, fashion, medicine, technology, the arts, entertainment, and much else besides. They disseminate values that shape people in small places, and that culture-shaping influence is usually unilateral. People in Pepperell know something about New York City, but people in New York City know nothing about Pepperell. I'm thankful for the leaders and ministries that have recognized the strategic influence of cities. I see a lot of wisdom in their way of thinking. But I want to push back in several ways. (We'll examine their view even more carefully in chapter twelve.)

I'm concerned that this particular kind of strategic thinking does not become our *only* way of thinking. I'll suggest in this chapter that *strategic* doesn't always mean what we think. As we reflect deeply on the gospel of Jesus Christ, we can see how its message and priorities might send us to the small places and shape our ministry there in seemingly *unstrategic* ways. So before you pack your bags to move to the city, please keep reading.

A LAVISH GOSPEL

One of the most precious things about the gospel is that it often seems so *un*strategic by worldly metrics. The gospel is lavish—you might even say it's *wasteful*. Think of Jesus' parable of the lost sheep. A shepherd leaves ninety-nine of his sheep in the open country and seeks the one that's lost until he finds it. Then he puts it on his shoulders and comes home and parties with his friends and neighbors. That's a lot of searching and celebrating for just one ordinary sheep. In one sense, the shepherd's actions aren't very strategic; they're *inordinate*. In fact, Jesus' parables of the lost sheep, the lost coin, and the lost son in Luke 15 emphasize the lengths people will go to find what's missing. The woman turns all the lights on, sweeps the whole house, and seeks "diligently" until she finds the coin. The father runs toward his son in an undignified fashion and then throws him a big party with the best food, music, and dancing. Consider also the famous episode involving Jesus' friend Mary soon before Jesus' death:

> Six days before the Passover, Jesus therefore came to Bethany, where Lazarus was, whom Jesus had raised from the dead. So they gave a dinner for him there. Martha served, and Lazarus was one of those reclining with him at table. Mary therefore took a pound of expensive ointment made from pure nard, and anointed the feet of Jesus and wiped his feet with her hair. The house was filled with the fragrance of the perfume. (John 12:1-3)

Mary's ointment was worth close to a year's wages. Imagine blowing $50,000 at one dinner party. You would not be commended for your prudence and common sense. In fact, in this instance Judas was quick to point out that Mary could have sold the ointment and given the money to the poor. Though Judas had ulterior motives, what he said does make some sense. But Jesus commended Mary's lavish gift. The call-and-response of the gospel is a lavish divine love evoking a lavish human response (Luke 7:36-50).

In one sense, love itself is not very strategic. Anyone who's ever been a parent understands this. Loving parents live on repeat. They tell their children a thousand times not to touch the wall socket; they change their diapers a thousand times and kiss a thousand boo-boos; they clean up messes, repeat words of love, and retell the same stories over and over again. Good parents regularly "waste" time with their kids, coloring and hosting imaginary tea parties and playing silly games when they could be accomplishing more important things. All that energy and attention squandered on just one little person is called love.

The gospel proclaims God's own extravagant, sacrificial love, which comes to people not because of what they can contribute (in leveraging influence with others) but because of what they *can't* contribute (in saving themselves). It may seem inordinate for God to surrender his own Son to death in order to purchase for himself, well, *you*. But that's gospel love. And it's precisely as each one of us comes to experience this inordinate love that we're changed forever. The apostle Paul had this very experience. After his conversion on the Damascus Road, he came to see that the Son of God "loved me and gave himself for me" (Galatians 2:20), and that Christ Jesus had made Paul his own (Philippians 3:12). Christ's love became the defining force and motivation of Paul's life (2 Corinthians 5:14).

Jesus himself seems often to have been unstrategic about the people he loved. Luke's Gospel particularly emphasizes his interest in the marginal, the oppressed, the outsider, the *non*-influential. He appears to have focused largely on underprivileged people: "the peasants and the fishermen, rural wage laborers and tenant farmers, day laborers and serfs, artisans and traders, beggars and prostitutes."[3] The apostle Paul followed Jesus' pattern of relating to all types of people, including those who didn't seem to have much to offer. "I am under obligation both to Greeks and to barbarians, both to the wise and to the foolish" (Romans 1:14).

It may seem odd to cite Paul as an example of being unstrategic since those who commend city-focused ministry often ground their approach in Paul's own ministry strategy. It's commonly held that Paul focused his efforts exclusively on strategic cities, the centers of commerce, arts, and government, influencing influencers, expecting that gospel influence would radiate out from those cities into surrounding regions.

But it's worth questioning this view. Did Paul target great cities because they were filled with affluent, influential creators of culture? The evangelical New Testament scholar Eckhard Schnabel, who has written several important books on early Christian mission, doesn't think so. "Paul did not have a mission strategy that sought to initiate (or consolidate) missionary work by establishing contacts with the powerful elites of the cities or provinces in which he preached the gospel."[4] Of course, Paul did speak to some influential people, but it's equally clear that he regularly associated with "nobodies." His strategy (if it can even be called that) seems to have been to engage whoever would listen. His ministry in one particular Greek city (Corinth) seems to have resulted mostly in a church of nobodies: "For consider your calling, brothers: not many of you were wise according to worldly standards, not many were powerful, not many were of noble birth" (1 Corinthians 1:26).

To be clear, I'm not saying that all strategic thinking is the opposite of gospel love. I believe God sometimes calls some of his people to big-picture thinking, to consider how to influence the wider culture and the greatest number of people possible. I'm thankful for the humble, visionary leaders he has gifted to do such thinking in our generation. I'm not saying that all strategizing of that sort is bad. But there's a lavishness, an extravagance, a prodigality at the heart of the gospel that can subvert our conceptions of what is strategic. I'm saying that the lavish nature of the gospel may be uniquely expressed through seemingly unstrategic ministries in seemingly unstrategic churches in seemingly unstrategic places.

A LAVISH MINISTRY

What's strategic for the kingdom of God isn't always the same as what's strategic for the world. Thinking about this on a personal level is helpful. Call to mind someone you know and love. What's the best ministry strategy for reaching that person with the gospel? It's certainly not leaving them and going elsewhere to influence other people who will eventually influence them. In fact, the best strategy is not very *strategic* at all. It's going deep in friendship, listening a lot, spending time together, serving and being served. It's genuinely caring and praying over the course of many years and speaking gospel words when you have the opportunity.

Similarly, a call to a small, unstrategic place is actually the most strategic way of reaching that particular place. The best way to reach Pepperell with the gospel is to live and minister for a long time in Pepperell—not Boston. Reaching Pepperell with the gospel requires a heavy Pepperell presence: loving Pepperell people, eating in Pepperell restaurants, investing in Pepperell schools, shopping in Pepperell stores, caring about Pepperell problems, participating in Pepperell celebrations, sharing in Pepperell sadnesses. Of course, a lifetime in Pepperell may not seem very strategic. My town is not exactly a hub of fashion, commerce, and cultural influence. It's fair to say that our movers and shakers don't move and shake quite as well as city people. But the nature of the gospel endorses a long presence in Pepperell (and small places everywhere). The lavishness of the gospel gives God's people permission and encouragement to love and serve uninfluential, unstrategic people in forgotten places. There are loads of people in my congregation who are just *normal* people. I'm one of them. They're not going to change the world any more than I am. But the logic of the gospel is that God was willing to give his own Son for them. Can I deem them not important enough to merit my time, attention, and love?

I long for us to see that the lavish nature of the gospel is best modeled by a lavish ministry—and lavish ministries flourish uniquely in small places because small places by definition lack influence and are considered unimportant. There aren't as many trend-setting, world-changing people there, and yet the gospel is still for these places.

Can big city churches full of government workers and CEOs and college professors embody lavish gospel love? Absolutely. I've ministered in those churches and I've seen it happen. But the very *smallness* of small places allows the generosity of the gospel to shine through gospel ministry with particular clarity. The more podunk the place, the more clearly the world will see God's prodigality in blessing it with a servant-hearted church, a gospel-centered pastor, and leaders committed to its good. When the answer to the question, Why is your church there? couldn't possibly be to get rich, become famous, gain influence, or maximize growth potential (all reasons the world understands), there's a precious opportunity for the gospel's logic to be heard: because God offered his Son for the people who live here.

This is what makes the church stand out from other institutions. Because God loves people everywhere, he calls his church to be present everywhere. Thus his church must be in places big and small in order to be the church.[5] As Brad Roth notes, other organizations aren't like this. Shopping malls, for instance, exist only in cities and suburbs because their purpose is commercial. But, as Roth puts it, "the rural church represents Christ's commitment to be among all people everywhere, regardless of the value attributed to them by global centers of power."[6]

LIVING LAVISHLY

How exactly your particular small-place church will become see-through to reveal the lavish gospel of Jesus Christ isn't for me to say. It's for you to discern over time, through prayer and the guidance of God's Holy Spirit, as the gospel has its shaping effect.

In recent years my church has discovered a love for seniors. It's happened without any planning on our part. One of our mission partners serves full-time in nursing homes, hearing the stories of eighty- and ninety-year-olds and sharing the gospel with hundreds of them every year. Numerous women in our church work and volunteer at the local senior center. God has led others in our congregation to form a choir that sings for shut-ins and those in hospice care, and he has called still others to spend time with those who are sick and dying, to care for those with dementia, and to provide rides for seniors. He has opened relationships for me with elderly neighbors and grown friendships with the leaders of our community senior center. As we've noticed this happening, our church has begun to explore additional ways to serve the older generation in our town.[7]

Our impulse to love seniors flows from and displays a lavish gospel. Church-growth experts would tell our church to focus on the young-family demographic. Of course, the gospel calls us to serve them too. But it's particularly exciting to imagine the potential of a church that's known for loving seniors. What does that communicate about a gospel that saves us not because of what we can give in return but because of what we can't? Aged widows on a pension won't bump up our budget. Those on death's door won't fill our ministry holes. Seniors have fewer years to influence others. They're less strategic—and that's the point. (That's not to say seniors have nothing to contribute: we've found great joy in learning from their experience and wisdom.)

Which people on the margins is your church already loving? Look around and see how God is already shaping your church with the contours of gospel love. Begin to prayerfully imagine how that love can be *inordinate*. The costly, extravagant, sacrificial love of the gospel will be seen through ministry in hospital rooms and beside death beds; among those who keep stumbling, repenting, and trying again; to those struggling with addiction or mental illness. As we've seen already, rural areas usually have fewer social service resources than cities; there are massive needs that God can use his church to meet.

A rural pastor in the American West told me about his neighbor Carter, who grew up in their town. Carter is typical of many small-town residents. His dad was abusive and spent the family's money on alcohol and cigarettes. When his parents divorced, Carter was raised by a neighbor who was more of a mother to him than his own mom. Following high school, Carter experimented with drugs and sex and got thrown out of the apartments of multiple girlfriends, often winding up on the couch of his adopted mom. After cleaning up and drying out, he'd find odd jobs to pay the rent for his mouse-infested trailer. Though he showed signs of promise working as an evening cook at the local bar, he eventually got busted for dealing drugs there, served a few months in jail, and took several years to pay off the fines. Carter's health isn't good, and he's lonely. His only close relationship is with his teen son, who treats him poorly.

Carter is not a strategic person. He will probably never become a community leader. It's unlikely he'll run any major institution or shape the broader culture through the arts, media, or commerce. His influence will likely be small and decidedly local. By the world's measure, he is an unimpressive person living in an unimpressive place. Who will minister the gospel to Carter? Any ministry to Carter will require the willingness to live where he lives—in a forgotten place. And that's exactly where my pastor friend and his church are living. They've provided lots of practical help for Carter, like car repairs and rent and gas money. He has friends in the church who check in on him, invite him to services, and pray with him. There's been much listening and counseling. Carter recently said he didn't know where he'd be without the support of the church.

Investing in Carter is a precious picture of the gospel. By serving and welcoming him into their gospel community, this small church is becoming a window that looks out on the gospel and the glory of God. That's not because Carter will never contribute anything to the kingdom. (In fact, he'll likely be much more effective in reaching his own town than a more impressive person from far away would be.) It's because, to most people, Carter is utterly unimpressive. His potential to reach many people and change the broader culture seems small. The chances that he can pay back this church in any substantial way are minimal. For this reason, it's especially clear that *only the gospel* will motivate God's people to keep serving and loving Carter.

I once watched a video testimonial from a rural pastor who said, "People in rural North America deserve truth, and committed shepherding, and . . . discipling as much as any other place."[8] Of course, I agree that rural people aren't less deserving of gospel ministry than city-dwellers. But it's inadequate and unhelpful to ground ministry (whether rural or urban) in human deserving. The danger is that if we come to feel that certain people are undeserving, our love will run out. We'll stop ministering to them. When our ministry is grounded not in human deserving but in God's character embodied and expressed in the gospel, we have a deeper, more enduring source for ministry. God pursues *inordinately*. In fact, he pursues us even while we're still his enemies.

When our seemingly unstrategic ministries in seemingly unstrategic places to "nobodies" like Carter are lived along the grain of the gospel, they display the character of God. A whole life lived in, and a whole ministry dedicated to, a small, unimportant place embodies precious aspects of the gospel that a highly successful, influencing-the-influencers ministry never can.

I'm grateful that God calls college presidents, art directors, and investment bankers to himself. When Paul told the church in Corinth that "not many of you were wise according to worldly standards, not many were powerful, not many were of noble birth," he clearly implied that there were *some* wise, powerful, and well-born among them (see Romans 16:23). If every Christian lives next door to Carter, we'll never minister to the Federal Reserve chairmen of the world. That would be a tragedy. When God converts an educated, privileged influencer, he displays unique and wondrous features of his character and his gospel. He demonstrates, among other things, that he's more precious than all the many privileges the important person previously possessed (see Philippians 3:3-11). But God's glory is too multifaceted to be fully displayed in the conversions of investment bankers or Carters alone. The church will be a window to his worth as we go everywhere, to everyone.

BIRMINGHAM PEOPLE HAVE SOULS

By his thirties, the nineteenth-century churchman John Henry Newman was already a dominant religious figure in England. He was one of the leaders of the Oxford Movement, which sought to reform the Anglican Church. Because he was enormously influential, his conversion to the Catholic Church in 1845 sent shock waves throughout England. Together with his conversion came a relocation from Oxford to Birmingham. Reflecting on Newman's move, the American pastor Eugene Peterson wrote that Newman

> abandoned Oxford and its elegant surroundings, his place of intellectual prestige and religious influence, and chose to spend the rest of his life in the Birmingham of belching steel furnaces, teaching boys in an ugly neighborhood where no one read books. Newman in Birmingham? It was like Einstein leaving Princeton to start a school for street kids in the Bronx.[9]

Why did Newman make such an unstrategic move? There were many factors, but Newman reveals an important one in a short note he wrote in 1864. He had been invited by an Englishman, George Talbot, to preach to an important, educated congregation in the Piazza del Popolo in Rome. Talbot was clearly proud of his impressive congregation. In his note responding to the invitation, Newman explained his reasons for declining:

The Oratory, Birmingham: July 25, 1864.

Dear Monsignore Talbot,—I have received your letter, inviting me to preach next Lent in your Church at Rome to "an audience . . . more educated than could ever be the case in England." However, Birmingham people have souls; and I have neither taste nor talent for the sort of work which you cut out for me. And I beg to decline your offer.

I am, yours truly, JOHN H. NEWMAN.

"Birmingham people have souls." Of course, Oxford people and residents of Rome do too. But to deeply believe that "Birmingham people have souls" could free a person to be able to hear God's call—if God extended it—away from a center of influence and toward possible obscurity. It could lead to choices as surprising as declining Rome and departing Oxford. It could cause a person to invest deeply, for a long time, in uncultured, uneducated, uninfluential people. Such a move would express something of the gospel itself. Eugene Peterson asks, "Newman in Birmingham?" And we might ask, "Jesus in Nazareth?" "Jesus on his way to Jerusalem?" "Jesus hanging on the cross?" That's the heart of the gospel.

I'll never forget attending a farewell celebration for a small-town pastor I love and admire. He and his wife had exercised a wise and sacrificial ministry in their community and congregation for over thirty years, though few outside their town knew their names. During those years this pastor could often be found visiting at hospital bedsides or down on his knees, speaking with children at eye level, interested in their lives. The highlight of the farewell celebration came as person after person shared stories of how this couple had pointed them to Jesus and freed them for joy. It was evident that for many years the gospel had been big in this small place. The love of a faithful pastor pouring himself out for a small congregation over three decades of ministry seemed like an echo of the woman who pours a year's wages onto Jesus' feet, the shepherd who celebrates his one sheep, and the God who sends his Son to die for us.

How much is it worth to rescue one person for eternity? It's worth a lifetime of ministry. We began this chapter pondering the question of whether, with only (at most) forty or fifty years of productive ministry available to each of us, we ought to focus our ministry on influencing influencers. God will call some of us to that kind of ministry. It's a good way to invest a life. But remember that Jesus himself had only three years of ministry, and he chose to spend most of them in the small towns and villages of Galilee.[10] He shows us it's not a waste.

6

Small Is Usually Better Than We Think

THESE DAYS MOST PEOPLE prefer big things to small things. We're willing to pay extra for more square footage, more legroom, and a larger screen. This cultural preference also applies to the size of the communities we live in; many have voted with their feet by moving to cities and suburbs.

But despite our cultural preference for bigger things, most American churches are small. The National Congregations Study found that in 2012 the median Sunday morning church attendance in the United States was 60 people.[1] Forty-three percent of American churches had fewer than 50 regular participants, 67 percent had fewer than 100 regular participants, and 87 percent had fewer than 250.[2] Moreover, many of these small churches are located in small places. Robert Wuthnow notes that "there are more churches per capita in less populated areas than there are in more heavily populated places."[3] A Barna study found that in New England, where I live, 40 percent of churchgoing Christians live in small towns or rural areas (though, of course, some commute to urban or suburban churches).

If there's a bottom rung on the ladder of importance and prestige among churches, it's surely occupied by small churches in small places. No one is clambering to visit or profile these churches or to discover their secret sauce for ministry success. Their pastors don't receive speaking invitations and aren't invited to sit on the boards of major Christian organizations. Perhaps even more worryingly, surveys show that small churches in small places aren't particularly attractive to the next generation of pastors.[4] Sometimes these churches seem to be altogether forgotten by writers and church leaders. One church-planting expert suggests that to start a church there should be at least fifty to one hundred adults before going public. As Glenn Daman notes, that precludes almost all rural-church planting![5]

But the feeling that small churches in small places are somehow inferior goes even deeper: it's sometimes shared by the very ones *leading* these churches. Small church pastors want to be successful, and our broader culture's preferences have shaped a version of success that entails churches getting *big*. It's a powerful narrative, sustained by the attention lavished on the large, innovative churches and their gifted pastors. Small-town, small-church ministers may look at big churches in big places and envy them, feeling dissatisfied with their own place and ministry. At pastors' conferences it's common to be asked, "How big is your church?"

If you minister in a small church, how do you feel about answering that question? Have you ever counted babies in utero or people who visited one service six years ago in your final tally? It may be that we've bought into a cultural preference that denigrates our own ministries and congregations.

PRIZING THE SMALL

We should ask ourselves whether our preference for big things is shaped more by our culture or by the gospel. It turns out that even though the gospel is very big in all the ways we've been discussing, it does not disdain what is small and unimpressive. In fact, it delights in small things. The gospel announces that the Son of God came as a baby and gathered twelve disciples ("uneducated, common men" according to Acts 4:13) during his brief life and ministry. The Bible's remnant theology shows us that often it's the few (the remnant) who trust and follow God, not the many. In fact, that very remnant theology climaxes in the gospel, which proclaims that ultimately there is just one faithful man, Jesus Christ, and that salvation is achieved through his one death and the end-time general resurrection begins with his one resurrection. Jesus said, "The kingdom of heaven is like a grain of mustard seed that a man took and sowed in his field. It is the smallest of all seeds. . . . The kingdom of heaven is like leaven that a woman took and hid in three measures of flour" (Matthew 13:31-33).

In Jesus' day, the declaration of a hidden kingdom was at best bewildering. The kingdom was supposed to arrive so publicly that you couldn't possibly miss it. Think lightning rather than a lightning bug. But Jesus never backed away from his teaching of a seed-sized kingdom, and his church continues to affirm it in word and deed. Each time the church receives the Lord's Supper, we declare our gratitude for what is surprisingly small. We share together an absurdly miniature feast—a tiny fragment of bread and a tiny sip of wine, neither sufficient to satisfy our physical appetite. The feast's smallness is its point. It reminds us that what we have is real but not fully realized, that we're still awaiting the great future messianic banquet where we'll feast to our heart's content. The bread and cup are a foretaste of the feast. We're grateful for what we have, even as we groan for more.

We gather as God's redeemed people around this tiny meal. We live in a mustard-seed kingdom. We remain hopeful in a desperate world because of a solitary death and resurrection. Through the gospel, God rewrites our valuations of big and small. We honor Jesus' teaching to love small children ("little ones") since their worth isn't in their size or maturity but in God's pleasure. As the Puritan Richard Sibbes wrote, "It is Christ that raises the worth of little and mean places and persons. Bethlehem was the least . . . and yet not the least; the least in itself, not the least in respect that Christ was born there."[6] In gospel logic, small is often very good.

And yet, as so often in the Bible, God holds together the things we separate. The gospel's surprising valuing of small doesn't mean that big is bad. After all, the baby Jesus grew into a man, the resurrection of the one man leads to the resurrection of many, and the Lord's Supper will become the lavish end-time banquet. Yes, the kingdom comes like a mustard seed, but "when it has grown it is larger than all the garden plants and becomes a tree, so that the birds of the air come and make nests in its branches" (Matthew 13:32). Christ will conquer every enemy, God will put all things in subjection under Christ's feet, and God will be all in all (1 Corinthians 15:24-28). That's a good kind of big.

Moreover, the gospel's valuing of small doesn't mean small is *always* good. In Jesus' parable of the minas, the servant who invests his master's money and makes a sizable return is praised, while the servant with only the mina he was initially given is rebuked. His small return reflects a wicked heart (Luke 19:11-27). If a church is small because its life is being choked out by poor preaching and leadership, that's a bad kind of small. If it's small because there's no sense of mission and no evangelism and no compelling vision of what God can do or if it's small because the leaders are lazy and comfortable with the *status quo*, that's the wrong kind of small.

The shape of the gospel doesn't imply that big is always bad or that small is always good. The gospel is more realistic and more nuanced than that—but no less surprising for it. The nature of the gospel shows that small is not *always*, *inevitably* worse than big (contrary to the prevailing view of our culture). Small can be very good. We already believed that about big. But small is probably better than we think. God delights in choosing small, unimpressive things in order to magnify his greatness and glory.

THE GIFTS OF A SMALL PLACE

As we allow the gospel to reshape our view of small places, we'll begin to see *opportunities* where previously we saw only inferiority.

Here's an unexpected gift: in small places, more of life is onstage. Far more small-town residents say they know almost all their neighbors, compared to residents of larger, metropolitan areas.[7] In larger places, your home life—or your decision to blare music in your car or cut someone off in traffic—is considered anonymous. It's backstage behavior.[8] But in small towns these things are noticed, known, and shared. The downside is that if you say or do something dishonoring to Christ, it will likely be repeated by the local rumor mill. You can scuttle your reputation very quickly. This was in my mind recently after I expressed frustration on the phone to my local tax guy, who had been slow about preparing my taxes, pushing me right to the filing deadline. (I like to be organized and well ahead of time.) The reason I picked up the phone a second time and apologized to him for not being more understanding was mainly because the Holy Spirit convicted me of the need to confess my sinful response but also because I cared about preserving my reputation and the reputation of my church. It matters a lot.

However, this "onstage" feature of small-town life isn't all negative: it also works the other way around. "Do things in public you want people to see," says Donnie Griggs. "I try to go out of my way to be present in meaningful ways when the town is celebrating or mourning. I want them to know I'm not living in a church office between Sunday mornings."[9]

The smallness of your small place means you'll be recognized around town if you make even a minimal effort to be present. As you come to be known and trusted, you'll be asked for help and counsel. For years my young children and I took our trash to the transfer station every Saturday morning. (You should hear us singing "The Dump Song," an original Witmer musical creation.) One Saturday, Roland, a candidate for town selectman, stood in front of the plastics recycling asking for votes. We spoke briefly, which led to a friendship and further partnership in service to the town. Over the course of many other Saturday mornings, my children and I became friends with one of the transfer station employees. When his daughter was planning her wedding and didn't have a minister for the ceremony, Paul told her he knew one. I met regularly with the couple and led their wedding service with many community members in attendance. Who knew recycling could be so fruitful?

Other gospel opportunities have come to us in the context of everyday life. Our kids love the little dog that a man in our neighborhood walks past our house twice a day. As we engaged our neighbor in conversation while our kids played with his dog, a friendship grew. One day he asked me to lead the funeral of his grown son, who had died from cancer, and later he and his wife joined a Bible study group that meets weekly in our home.

The smallness of our context gives us an outsized influence. One Christian worker in a poor, rural area of the American South notes that, in his experience, ministry to children in small towns "hits the community as a whole quicker and more profoundly" than in urban and suburban settings. A West Virginia pastor told me he knows the mayor and 150 small business owners in his county; there's no building in town he won't be welcomed in. A New Hampshire pastor in a town of three hundred said that 5 to 10 percent of the town attends his church. To achieve that level of influence in a city, a church would need to draw fifty thousand to one hundred thousand attendees.

And living as a Christian in a small place is advantageous not just for mission from your church but for relationships within it. When churchgoers in small, nonmetropolitan communities are compared with those in big cities, more of the small-place church-goers have a sizable number of close friends in their congregation. That's probably because the smallness of their town allows for more interactions throughout the course of the week.[10]

By showing us that small isn't necessarily bad, that God often chooses to work through small people in small ways, the gospel forms people and churches who see the opportunities presented by small places. Though it's a countercultural instinct, we slowly come to see that small is better than we think.

THE GIFTS OF A SMALL CHURCH

Of course, there are small churches in big places and big churches in small places. Still, churches in small places do tend to be small. And if the gospel has made us okay with smallness, we'll have eyes to see the many benefits it brings. We'll embrace the strengths *and* weaknesses of our smallness.

While writing this book I lived alone for a week in the cottage of friends on the Antrim Coast of Northern Ireland, without a phone, internet, or car. On Sunday morning, a nearby sheep farmer offered to drive me to church. There were one hundred people in the congregation that morning, and it was the final Sunday for Eric, an eighty-year-old man, who had attended the church for many years and was moving away to be closer to family. The pastor announced Eric's departure and then spoke to him directly, encouraging him. The congregation sang a song the pastor had chosen with Eric in mind. Eric was mentioned throughout the rest of the service and when it ended, the entire congregation joined hands and sang a song of blessing and farewell.

I was deeply encouraged by this. This was a small church that wasn't afraid of *being* a small church. The strengths of small churches are intimacy and involvement; they feel like a family, and the service of every family member is needed and valued.[11] This little Antrim church was loving each other and displaying the beauty of the gospel in ways a church of three thousand people could never do.

Another major benefit enjoyed by small churches in small places is the awareness of their own weaknesses. This doesn't always feel like a benefit, but it is. With just forty-five regular Sunday morning attenders (or 85 or 145), there's less that's outwardly impressive about their gatherings. The meeting places are usually more humble. Small congregations don't often get to enjoy professional musicians or see professional-grade graphic design wherever they look or hear preaching that generates thousands of downloads online the following week. They don't experience the natural pleasure and encouragement of welcoming new visitors on Sunday morning as often. With many older people in the congregation, there is more accumulated wisdom but also the inevitable struggles with health, energy, and willingness to try new things.

Beyond these realities, there's an ever-present awareness of fragility. A small church in a small place will know that if a few of the regular attenders move out of town or opt for a more exciting church across town with lots of programs and excellent music, their places may not be filled. If even a few people stop giving, the church may not meet its budget. Many small churches are just a few steps from having to close their doors for good.

Faced with these realities, a small church in a small place will find there are some things it can work to improve. It can patiently, prayerfully grow toward God-glorifying excellence in its facilities, music, pulpit ministry, and small groups. It might do these things and experience genuine excitement when more people come. Perhaps its numbers will even double, say from forty-five to ninety people. But one day it will realize that it's still a small church in a small place. At that point, it will have an important choice to make. Either it will reject its own smallness, or it will reject the cultural assumption that small is usually bad. Instead, it will entrust its size and growth to God.

Some small churches and their ministers will become dissatisfied with who they are. This may manifest itself in a restless striving to implement the latest program from some big church in some big place. Or it may settle into a long, slow simmer of discontentment, endless tinkering, and yearning for something more and better. I once participated in a gathering of fellow small-town and rural pastors. We were a bunch of no-names but passionate lovers of Jesus and people. We met in a wealthy suburban megachurch with a worship band good enough to sell out concerts, a sound board as big as a dining room table, and high-tech projection screens. I've wondered since whether this was a parable of the contemporary American church: a group of small-place, small-church pastors, lifted out of our own contexts and set down, wide-eyed, in an impressive facility that bore little resemblance to what we knew, quietly yearning for the resources, personnel, and excellence of a bigger place.

There's a better way to respond to your small church's manifest weakness and fragility. At first it may seem paradoxical. It's to long *more* for the numerical growth of your church but to need it *less*. God calls every small-town, small-church member and leader to this.

Plead with God for conversions. Ask him for a miraculous, sur- prising work in your small place for the good of lost souls and the glory of his name, to show that he can bring life from the dead and something from nothing (Romans 4:17). Some of my friends have experienced enormous, inexplicable conversion growth in their small-town churches. If you don't believe God can do this in your town—if you've never even asked him for it or aren't *persevering* in asking him—confess your lack of faith to God together with any apathy, laziness, or selfish *status quo* comfort you may have. Let's be honest: while it's certainly true that some small-church ministers desire bigger churches for the wrong reasons (to stoke their pride or soothe their fears), it's equally true that other small-church ministers become reconciled to their churches staying small for the wrong reasons (lack of faith, fear of change, comfort with the way things are). They need to begin longing and praying for numerical growth.

Even as you plead with God to reach your town and swell your ranks with people who don't know him, seek to receive—as a gift from God—the manifest weakness of your small church in your small place. Don't run from it. Receive it. Every church, big or small, urban or rural, is utterly dependent on its Head. Without Christ's sustaining grace, no church can last or have any lasting impact. Every church must receive and reckon with this knowledge.

But the particular gift God gives to small churches in small places is that their weakness is so evident. Your weakness cannot hide behind a professional worship band, a beautiful new building, or the excitement generated by filling up a huge sanctuary. It can't hide behind a large budget surplus or deep cash reserves. And if your small, unimpressive church is plopped down in the middle of an equally small, unimpressive town, you will also be denied the pleasure of what E. B. White called "the excitement of participation"—the sense of belonging to something "unique, cosmopolitan, mighty, and unparalleled."[12] As a small church in a small place, you won't have access to the illusion of greatness through proximity. Your church's weakness will be evident to you and to everyone else—and this is God's gift.

In *The Bruised Reed*, the Puritan pastor Richard Sibbes reflected on the nature of weakness. He said,

> As a mother is tenderest to the . . . weakest child, so does Christ most mercifully incline to the weakest. Likewise he puts an instinct into the weakest things to rely upon

> something stronger than themselves for support. . . . The
> consciousness of the church's weakness makes her willing
> to lean on her beloved, and to hide herself under his wing.[13]

Even as we pray for surprising conversion growth, will our manifest weakness and fragility make our little congregations willing to lean on Christ and hide "under his wing"? Will it lead us to frequent, fervent prayer for our churches and towns? Our churches (and every church) will minister to people not by showing them how big and impressive we are, but by displaying the greatness of the God who says, "I am the first and I am the last; besides me there is no god" (Isaiah 44:6). Can we long *more* for the numerical growth of our churches while needing it *less*?

The smallness of our small-place churches may be God's way of making us see-through to the gospel. In *Making Sense of God*, Tim Keller shares an important insight: the biblical theme of God choosing those who are marginal and powerless isn't just because the biblical writers loved underdogs.

> It is because the ultimate example of God's working in the
> world was Jesus Christ, the only founder of a major religion
> who died in disgrace, not surrounded by all of his loving
> disciples but abandoned by everybody whom he cared about,
> including his Father. . . . Jesus Christ's salvation comes to
> us through his poverty, rejection, and weakness.[14]

Weak churches may be uniquely able to display a gospel that comes in weakness.

By no means should we aim for musical mistakes in the service or sermons that fall flat! But if these things happen, we shouldn't run from our weakness. We can consider them a reminder that we receive God's salvation by admitting our own poverty. We can allow God's strength to work through weakness, his love to shine through flaws, so that even the wrong notes are folded into a better song that makes much of God and his gospel. The smallness of our place, the unimpressiveness of our churches, even our own inadequacies and failings are themselves an expression of the gospel we proclaim. The medium reflects the message—the good news that God offers salvation to all people based not on their greatness but his grace.

The gospel allows small-church ministers and members to need rapid church growth less while praying for it more. We don't need the validation church growth offers or the secure salary it promises. The gospel provides us with validation and security. It makes us more restless to see others embrace it and simultaneously more patient when they don't.[15]

BIG AND SMALL IN THE MINISTRY OF WILLIAM GRIMSHAW

William Grimshaw is mostly unknown today. Born in 1708 in a small, agricultural parish in Lancashire, England, he graduated from Cambridge University, later describing his Cambridge years as a period of learning to drink, swear, and become "as vile as the worst." The unconverted Grimshaw was ordained in the Church of England, eventually settling in the tiny town of Todmorden, where he ministered for eleven years. During that decade he married, had two children, and then became a young widower when his wife, Sarah, died. Her death cast him into a period of intense distress, loneliness, and depression.

A year and a half later, Grimshaw came to the major turning point of his life. While visiting a friend, he happened to see a volume of John Owen's *The Doctrine of Justification by Faith* lying on a table and began to read. Owen's book helped him finally to understand and receive the gospel. Later, he reported to a friend, "I was now willing to renounce myself, every degree of fancied merit and ability, and to embrace Christ only for my all in all. O what light and comfort did I now enjoy in my own soul, and what a taste of the pardoning love of God!"[16]

In 1742, Grimshaw was appointed the minister of Haworth in Yorkshire. He ministered there for the next twenty-one years, until his death of a fever in 1763. He came to a very small church in a very small place, and while the place stayed small, the church didn't.

Haworth had about two thousand residents and was by all accounts a rough, uncivilized place.[17] J. C. Ryle relates the humorous legend that "when the first carriage came to Haworth the villagers brought out hay to feed it, under the idea that it was an animal!" The town had primitive sanitary arrangements that led to sickness, a low life expectancy, and a high death rate.[18] John Newton, who was a friend of Grimshaw, said that when Grimshaw arrived the people of Haworth "had little more sense of religion than their cattle, and were wild and uncultivated like the mountains and rocks which surrounded them."[19] The church was tiny, with only a handful of people regularly receiving the Lord's Supper. It was a decidedly unpromising place for pastoral work.

But God had big plans for the small church. Grimshaw was a man gripped by the gospel. He preached clear, powerful sermons and began visiting his parishioners in their homes. Ryle says there was "a life, and fire, and reality, and earnestness" about his public ministry that seemed "a totally different thing from what it was in other churches."[20] Soon his ministry began to have a striking effect:

> My church began to be crowded, insomuch that many were obliged to stand out of doors. Here, as in many places, it was amazing to see and hear what weeping, roaring, and agony, many people were seized with, at the apprehension of their sinful state and wrath of God.[21]

As word spread around the region of Haworth, people who were not receiving gospel preaching in their own churches began to travel miles to hear Grimshaw. In one eighteen-month period early in his ministry, at least 120 people were converted.[22] Just four years after he arrived in Haworth, four hundred to five hundred people were sharing Communion during the winter months, and twelve hundred in the summer months.[23] As the Great Awakening spread through England and beyond, Grimshaw welcomed John and Charles Wesley and George Whitefield to preach in his pulpit. The church building was enlarged in order to accommodate the large crowds.

Grimshaw's remarkable ministry in unremarkable Haworth can encourage small-place churches and ministers today. God did something in the tiny Haworth church that no one expected. He could have displayed something of his character and his gospel by allowing the church to stay small. Instead, he chose to display the stunning *power* of the gospel. Haworth became one of the centers of the Methodist revival as Grimshaw ministered extensively to a vast network of big and small places known as the "Great Haworth Round."[24] If God could do such a work in tiny, remote Haworth, can he not do it in small places today? Is there any place too small for God? Grimshaw's legacy encourages small-church, small-place ministers to long and pray for a big movement of God *more* than we already do.

But it simultaneously encourages us to need God's extraordinary work *less* and to be content if God chooses to give us something small. John Newton wrote,

> Though Mr Grimshaw often preached to great numbers, he was a no less attentive servant to a few. When any were willing to hear, he was willing to preach, and often cheerfully walked miles in the winter, in storms of wind, rain or snow, upon lonely unsheltered moors, to preach to a small company of aged, decrepit people in a cottage.[25]

Do we feel the same when numbers are low on a Sunday morning? Secure in the gospel, do we see the importance of individual souls and the unique blessing of small things? Could small actually be better than we think?

7

Slow Is Often Wiser Than We Think

I N 1824, A LITTLE MORE THAN SIXTY YEARS after William
Grimshaw's death, John Paton was born in the south of Scotland
to a gospel-loving stocking manufacturer and his godly wife.
While Grimshaw's life helps us consider the size of our ministries,
Paton's gives us perspective on their pace.

FAST AND SLOW IN THE MINISTRY OF JOHN PATON

In 1847, at the age of twenty-three, Paton was chosen to work in
the Glasgow City Mission. His ministry got off to a slow start;
after a year, only a handful of people were attending his meetings.
The directors of the Mission determined it would be best for
Paton to move to another district, but he pled to stay, feeling
there might be a breakthrough. The directors relented, granting
him another six months. And Paton was right: the following ten
years saw tremendous growth. Soon five hundred to six hundred
people were attending meetings each week. Paton led gatherings
almost every night of the week (with two on Sunday). Several
times his health broke down due to overwork.

During this decade of intense gospel labor, Paton felt an increasing call to the mission field. He was torn about leaving a fruitful, growing ministry. Friends urged him to continue what he was doing. But in 1858 he and his wife, Mary, sailed for the South Pacific as missionaries. Over the coming years it must have seemed to many that they had made a colossal mistake.

John and Mary landed on the island of Tanna (part of what is now the Republic of Vanuatu) on November 5, 1858. Only a few months later Mary died, followed two weeks later by their baby son Peter. Paton dug the two graves himself. This was the beginning of a grueling period of life and ministry. Over the next years his possessions were frequently stolen and he suffered numerous bouts of sickness. Two fellow missionaries were murdered in 1861. In 1862 he lost all his possessions and barely escaped from the island with his life, chased away by natives.

After four years on Tanna, Paton had seen virtually no spiritual fruit. A few natives seemed interested in the gospel, but Paton couldn't even be sure of that. The life and ministry of this thirty-eight-year-old childless widower had gone from big and fast in Glasgow to small and slow on a remote South Pacific island. But Missi, as the islanders called him, was undeterred. Over the next several years he traveled throughout Australia and Scotland, telling his story and raising money for the mission work. He remarried and had a child. The family returned to the South Pacific in 1866, this time settling on the island of Aniwa. Once again they commenced a faithful, courageous, persistent gospel ministry to the natives. By 1867, it had been nine years since he had first come to the South Pacific, and by God's providence, spiritual fruit came quickly that year. It started with a well.

The island of Aniwa had no permanent supply of fresh water, so Paton decided to dig a well. When he informed the natives of his plan, they believed he was going mad and responded, "O Missi! . . . Rain comes only from above. How could you expect our Island to send up showers of rain from below?"[1] Paton went ahead with his project. After digging down to twelve feet, a side collapsed. He shored it up and continued digging. He told the natives God would provide fresh water from the well. They still didn't believe him. Finally, at thirty feet, fresh water rushed in. The natives were flabbergasted. "Missi, wonderful, wonderful is the work of your Jehovah God! No god of Aniwa ever helped us in this way. The world is turned upside down, since Jehovah came to Aniwa!"[2] Paton announced that the entire island could draw water from his well—a princely gift. The chief then asked Paton's permission to preach a sermon the next Sunday. In the chief's sermon, he admitted that he and his people had often laughed at the things Paton said. "But from this day I believe that all he tells us about his Jehovah God is true. . . . For to-day we have seen rain from the earth. . . . The gods of Aniwa cannot hear, cannot help us, like the God of Missi. Henceforth I am a follower of Jehovah God."[3] The chief and others burned or buried their idols.

From 1868 until 1883 Paton experienced incredible spiritual blessing on Aniwa. The entire island converted to Christianity. Paton reported that "though no one was compelled to come to Church, every person on Aniwa, without exception, became an avowed worshipper of Jehovah God."[4] Until his death in 1907, Paton traveled the world telling his story and raising money for the work of the South Pacific mission.

PRIZING THE SLOW AND STATIONARY

Modern Western culture prefers fast to slow and movement to immobility. Slow is inconvenient, and stationary means stuck. We prize efficiency. We complain when the waiter doesn't bring our food promptly. We're antsy if our computer takes longer than half a second to load a web page. Movement means progress—toward a better house, a better neighborhood, a better job.

Sometimes ministers in small places share these cultural values without thinking about it. Perhaps we hear of urban churches planting new churches multiple times each year, and we feel panicky, like we're not doing enough. We can't even get a new website completed in six months or decide on the color of the toolshed behind the church! Or perhaps we hear of other pastors being courted by large city churches and feel stuck in our small church rather than grateful for our longevity there.

But we should ask ourselves whether our preference for the fast and mobile is formed by the gospel or by our culture. As we ponder the gospel, it shapes our approach to ministry. Of course, the gospel sometimes spreads rapidly. It can instantly change a person or a people group, as shown by the dramatic conversion of Paul on the Damascus Road, the Philippian jailer and his entire family, or the people of Aniwa in the South Pacific. When the gospel moves at light speed, it displays the remarkable, unstoppable power of God. When it spreads widely into new countries and cultures, it demonstrates that God is worthy of all peoples' worship. The high velocity of the gospel shows that fast isn't necessarily bad. The transcultural spread of the gospel shows that mobile isn't necessarily negative. But of course, in our speedy, transient culture we know that already.

The gospel challenges us much more in its affirmation that slow and stationary are sometimes okay and are often wiser than we think.

Recall how the gospel has affected your own life. You were saved the moment you first believed, but we can all identify areas of our lives in which progress has come slowly. My long battle with envy and slow growth in contentment have played out over time, not overnight. The gains have been hard-won, never hasty. The gospel often works more like a steady, soaking rain than a firehose spray. Ponder the way God has chosen to shape the history of redemption. Rather than bringing salvation through

Jesus all at once (as he could have done), God designed history to include *two* comings of Jesus separated by thousands of years (and counting). Jesus says the kingdom of God comes like a seed buried in the ground. Seeds aren't known for speed. In his wisdom and mercy, God sometimes acts slowly.

In fact, sometimes the gospel slows to such a crawl that it stops altogether and just *stays*. Over against a culture that defines success as constant, restless movement, the gospel tells us to stay. Jesus told his disciples that fruitfulness will require staying in place—remaining in him. "I am the vine; you are the branches. Whoever abides in me and I in him, he it is that bears much fruit, for apart from me you can do nothing" (John 15:5).

Moreover, the gospel declares that God himself stays put with us. He doesn't move on. His fidelity is complete. The "I in him" of John 15:5 recalls Jesus' words earlier in John's Gospel: "Whoever comes to me I will never cast out. . . . I will raise him up on the last day" (John 6:37, 44). Jesus is all in. He's not going anywhere.

THE PARADOXICAL TENSION OF FAST AND SLOW

We're faced here with another paradoxical tension. Our experience of God's love causes us to long for as *many* as possible to receive it as *quickly* as possible. It's good to pray for rapid gospel growth in small places, like the sudden, mass conversion of the Aniwan people. But we don't *need* God to do this, because our joy is not found in ministry success but in God's sure love.

That's what sustained John Paton during the four crushing years he spent on Tanna. When he fled the island in 1862, he spent part of the night hiding in a tree before it was safe to continue his escape. During his escape, Paton felt God's presence strongly. "Had I been a stranger to Jesus and to prayer, my reason would verily have given way, but my comfort and joy sprang out of these words, 'I will never leave thee, nor forsake thee; lo, I am with you alway!'"[5] Paton's son later wrote that this promise of Jesus' presence was Paton's source of "quietness and confidence in time of danger, and of his hope in the face of human impossibilities."[6]

The gospel strengthened Paton in lean years, even as it spurred him on to plead for plenty. It guarded him from being crushed when things stayed slow and small. It prevented him from getting lazy or faithless. It kept him humble when the ministry flourished. As these attitudes were manifest in Paton, his ministry became see-through to the gospel. His unstrategic choice to leave Glasgow to pour out his life for South Pacific islanders reflected something of Christ's own willingness to come for those who didn't deserve him and couldn't repay him. The first four years of suffering on Tanna spoke (to those with ears to hear) of a gospel that comes small and slow. The following years of triumphant plenty revealed (to those with eyes to see) a gospel that grows big and triumphs quickly in the end.

The gospel can shape us as it shaped Paton, delighting us with whatever aspects of God's character he chooses to reveal through the ministries he gives us. For some, God's gift will be a slow ministry in a slow place for our entire lives. Are we okay with that, or do we need something more?

Not long ago, a friend told me of a couple in his church who returned after twenty-seven years of missionary service in Papua New Guinea. They worked faithfully all those years, far from home, in order to translate the Scriptures into the language of a village of only six hundred people. There were no stories of mass conversions as a result of their work. But can we see the beauty and gospel shape of their ministry? It requires long years to learn a new language in a faraway country and translate the Bible for a faraway tribe. Might it not also take that long to know a people and place much closer to home?

SLOW MINISTRY IN A SLOW PLACE

There's a common perception among both city and rural dwellers that the pace of life in small places is slower. That may or may not be true. People do in fact tend to walk faster in large cities, and transactions at the post office and gas station take longer in small towns.[7] But those are only a few indicators (from only a few studies), and we all know there are slow-moving people in the city and fast-moving people in small places. (I may qualify as one myself.)

Whether or not the pace of life is demonstrably slower in small places, it's significant that people who live in small places *perceive* it to be—and that they tend to like it that way.[8] Polls have shown that the desire for a slower pace is especially prevalent among those who live in small towns and rural areas.[9] Indeed, "towns-people revel in the daily sameness of it all—seeing the same neighbors, living in the same house they lived in as a child, and enjoying the same landscape."[10] It turns out that a slow gospel might be a uniquely good fit for ministry in small places.

The preference for a slow pace fits with the small-place values of familiarity, longevity, deep relationships, and trustworthiness. Such gifts come only gradually, over time. The gospel trains ministers to be okay with that, helping us to see that slow may be wiser than we think.

Over the past decade I've become friends with a leader in our town. Not long ago, in casual conversation, she asked me about our church's views on sexuality. That provided an opportunity to learn more about her views and to share my own, hopefully helping her see the possibility of a thoughtful view of sexuality that values people even as it yields to biblical authority and differs from the prevailing view of our culture. But that conversation was a decade in coming. It grew out of a mutual trust built on many interactions. Who knows where it will lead?

Contrast that conversation with the instinctive distrust I felt one evening as I was grilling burgers in my backyard and two men wearing neckties approached me from the street, eager to start a conversation and hand me literature. I didn't know or trust them; instead, I suspected they wanted something from me. I wanted to run into my house. Their approach was fast—and ineffective.

Ministry in small places tends to be slower than in large, fast-moving city or suburban churches. The sometimes-slow, sometimes-fast gospel of Jesus Christ teaches us to pray for fast growth and be okay when God chooses to go slow. My church is developing a vision for planting churches from our small town into other nearby small towns so that every town in our region has a vibrant, gospel-centered, community-engaged church. We'd love to see God accomplish this in the next few years, and we believe he can. We pray for revival. At the same time, we realize that given our resources and size, planting one new church every seven or eight years may be a good goal for us. If that's the pace God sets, we're okay with it. We've begun to talk about a hundred-year church-planting vision. If that's what it takes to get the job done, we'll pass the baton to a new generation when the time comes.

How can we encourage gospel fidelity that outlives the present generation and gospel passion that moves the vision forward after we're gone? By moving at God's speed. We'll flee laziness even as we enjoy the freedom of knowing that sometimes the gospel moves slowly.

A STABLE MINISTRY IN A SMALL PLACE

Some ministers buy into our culture's view that movement equals progress. Unfortunately, too many "mayfly pastors" come and go in the blink of a town's eye.[11] Wendell Berry's Jayber Crow says of the many ministers who spent time in his town that "Some were wise and some were foolish, but none, so far as Port William knew, was ever old."[12]

Ron Klassen and John Koessler identify the rapid turnover of pastors in small-town churches as one reason why many of these churches always remain in survival mode. The perpetual search for a new pastor makes it difficult to plan for the future.[13] Pastoral mobility also decreases pastoral influence. Particularly in small communities, respect is "the critical aspect of community leadership."[14] The informal leadership that ministers can have in a small place is granted over time, as they're seen to care for and invest in their place. A national study showed that small-town residents care more about community involvement, helpfulness, and volunteerism when forming opinions of their fellow residents than do the residents of cities and suburbs.[15] This suggests it's even more important for small-place pastors to stay, love, and serve over the long haul.

The gospel's call for stability and perseverance will lead some to stay in place. This staying isn't the result of having no other options: it's a choice.[16] We will remain because we love our people and place. What might be the result of generations of small-place ministers staying put, loving relentlessly, as God does, our rural landscapes of loss, our struggling small towns? The prophet Isaiah exalts God for doing wonderful things, "plans formed of old, faithful and sure" (Isaiah 25:1). The psalmist celebrates the steadfast love of the Lord that endures forever and his faithfulness that lasts to all generations (Psalm 100:4-5). This patient, divine love climaxes in the gospel of Jesus Christ. Long-abiding ministers and churches become see-through to this magnificent aspect of God's character.

UNSTRATEGIC, SMALL, SLOW

To adapt a phrase from Brad Roth, the gospel of Jesus Christ sends us to small places and tells us what to do once we get there. It challenges our cultural assumptions by commending the value of what is unstrategic, small, slow, and stable. It teaches us to practice "subversive geography," in which the value of any particular place does not depend on its proximity to the city but on "the fact that it is cherished by the God who created and sustains it" and "is rooted in its nearness to God."[17] The gospel shows that unstrategic, small, and slow ministries and churches can become see-through to the character of God embodied in the gospel and therefore successful in the way that counts most: displaying God's worth to the world. It also reminds us that the full display of God's character requires both rich and poor, influential and forgotten, big and small, fast and slow, mobile and stable. God and his gospel are that big.

Some of what we've seen in the last three chapters will resonate with those who have become alienated by our culture's addiction to size and speed. Against the focus on being strategic, many now call for authenticity and relationship. Against the push to get bigger, many now prize what is local and sustainable. Against the frenetic speed of Western life, many now value living simply and slowly. These values are evident in the slow-food movement and in the rise of local, farm-to-table culture. These movements embrace values affirmed in the gospel of Jesus Christ.

But the nourishing roots of a compelling vision for small-place ministry will never be cultural trends because cultural trends change over time. Rather, a vision for small-place ministry will grow from biblical and theological values, drawing on the nature of the gospel and the character of God. These will remain forever.

8

Fruitful Small-Place Ministry

THE CIRCLE AND THE ARROW

IN HIS ESSAY "Here Is New York," E. B. White described the strange gifts the famous city gave its citizens: the gift of loneliness and of privacy. Ironically, though New York City was "the greatest human concentrate on earth," its sheer size and volume of activity actually insulated its inhabitants. The city could swallow a thousand-foot ocean liner or a twenty-thousand-person convention: either could arrive in town and the vast majority of New York residents would never know about it. This feature of the city made every event within it optional for its inhabitants; each could "choose his spectacle." White wondered whether it was healthier to live in a community where you didn't have that insulation, where you inevitably knew and were affected by its triumphs and tragedies.

White's observations raise the importance of the scale of the communities where we live. We've seen already that there isn't just one kind of small town or rural area. Noting this variety, Robert Wuthnow suggests that "about the only generalization that can safely be ventured about small towns, it might seem, is that they are indeed small compared with most cities and suburbs."[1] That observation may seem inconsequential at first, but it matters a great deal.

In Wuthnow's words, "scale matters. . . . [S]mallness shapes social networks, behavior, and civic commitments."[2] Because small towns usually cover only a few square miles, residents share a view of the same lakes, rivers, fields, streets, and buildings. We have the same "visual horizon."[3] Because we know the same landmarks, we say things like, "Go past the place that used to be Dunkin' Donuts, over the bridge, then take a left by Kemp's Service Station." Sharing this local knowledge deepens our mutual belonging and permits a familiarity and security that we value highly.[4] We also share a common experience of what's happening in town. Small places can't simply absorb large (or even small) events and crises like E. B. White's New York City could. We don't get to choose what we tune into: it's right in front of us, and we're usually personally affected by it in some way. It matters to everyone in Pepperell how the site of the old paper mill will be redeveloped. It matters whether an old quarry on the road out of town is filled with construction waste. Even relatively small happenings are soon known by the entire town, whether it's the scuttlebutt of local politics or a personal crisis.

E. B. White also observed that the intimate scale of small towns can sometimes be replicated in the local, mixed-use neighborhoods of the great cities.[5] In fact, some have argued that the key dividing line among modern communities falls not between small towns and cities, but rather between small towns and cities on the one hand and suburbs on the other.[6] But Wuthnow argues that the size difference between small towns and big cities does shape how community is experienced in each. The resident of a close-knit city neighborhood still has a different experience of community than someone who lives in a small place.

THE CIRCLE AND THE ARROW

Wuthnow introduces a helpful metaphor for understanding the ways inhabitants of small towns and larger metropolitan areas think about and experience the places where they live. Residents of small towns, he says, sometimes drive out of town for trips or errands, but they tend to experience their community as a "bounded space." The town's municipal limits are a *circle* within which relationships and business occur. Residents of larger places, on the other hand (particularly suburbs) frequently come and go from their homes. "A person literally drives in one direction to work, another to the shopping mall, and yet another to church or school. Social relationships are scattered in those different directions."[7] Thus people from large places experience their communities more like an *arrow*.

This difference affects how people speak about their communities. When suburban residents describe their communities as family friendly, they usually mean they're racially diverse, have good amenities, and are convenient to an interstate or workplace. In other words, they're "a good location to come and go from."[8] When residents of small towns, on the other hand, speak of their communities as family friendly, they're referring to the safe, familiar, neighborly, and caring nature of these places. They're referring to working or shopping in town, going to church there, seeing their neighbors on a regular basis, and knowing the local banker or the schoolteachers personally.

The scale of a small place permits and encourages frequent overlap within the circle. The distinctive feature of small-town social networks is that people live quite close to one another and therefore, Wuthnow says,

> have opportunities to interact in multiple settings. The chances of knowing someone's name or having spoken to them in the past are greater among people who live in the

same small town than among people who live in different towns or different parts of a metropolitan area.[9]

Small-town residents see one another at church, at the post office, and on the sidelines of their kids' ballgames. When our son began kindergarten, we discovered that his teacher has a regular walking route past our house. (Over the years we've often had to restrain our excited children from interrupting her walks!) Surprisingly, the smallness of small places sometimes allows residents to have more ongoing interactions with people who are different from them than they would in the city. That's because small-town residents are "thrown together" in close proximity, whereas residents of bigger places often choose their friendship circles on the basis of shared lifestyles or interests.[10] In small communities with relaxed zoning laws, rich and poor may live next door to each other and interact on at least a superficial level.

Fruitful small-place ministry will reckon with the scale of our particular place and the culture it forms, seeing smallness not as a curse but a blessing and opportunity. Ministering within the circle of a small place rather than the arrow of a bigger place requires sensitivity to context. I'll suggest five ways we can take small-place realities into account as we seek to embody and express the gospel in small places.

BE A LOCAL CHURCH

Community matters to those who live within the circle of a small town. It should matter to small-town churches too. We should aim to be *local* churches. My small church in Pepperell has grown over the years through the arrival of people from neighboring towns who want biblical preaching and a gospel-centered community. We're thankful for their presence, and we love to serve them. But their arrival has been one of the factors leading us in recent years to consider our long-term vision. Do we want to become a large regional church, drawing our membership from many surrounding small towns? Some in the evangelical church have strongly urged small-town churches like ours to adopt a regional model. Consider the following quote from an article published by the National Association of Evangelicals in the early 1960s:

> It is a not entirely undesirable condition that thousands of our open country and village churches have been closed. There are declining populations in most rural communities. Improved transportation makes it possible for rural people to travel fifteen or more miles to church in less time than it takes many city people to go by bus or automobile to their churches. A general centralization of rural institutions in the larger villages and towns appears to be taking place today. It is only sensible to use the material things God has entrusted to us in the most efficient way. Instead of continuing to support small rural churches with missionary funds and part-time pastors who can provide only the most meager services for their people, we will do well whenever it is possible to merge these small churches into larger units which can carry on the work of Christ in a most effective and less costly way.[11]

In this model of rural ministry, the centralization of churches into larger units is the "most efficient way" of providing services in a less costly manner. This language is borrowed from the business world, and it's the near-opposite of the theological vision I've been developing in this book.

Perhaps this sounds like a vision of Walmart churches. In fact, that's what one evangelical leader has called for in response to the shrinking of many rural places:

> We need Wal-Mart churches: churches that will serve regional rural markets; churches that are friendly, carry lots of programs, are customer-driven rather than institution-driven;

churches that transcend the deep traditions of small communities and give permission to worship without alienating family histories and relationships.[12]

More recently, a small-town pastor of a large church suggested that "rural churches . . . need to think regionally," focusing on a county rather than a town in order to grow. He notes that since rural people are willing to drive for play, work, and the hardware store, we should expect them to do the same for church.[13]

Our church disagrees. We have no desire to "transcend the deep traditions of small communities." In fact, we hope to sink *deeper* into the life of our town. As Winn Collier's fictional pastor Jonas McAnn says of his ministry and town, "I want to preach sermons that would only fit in Granby. I want to live a life that wouldn't make much sense anywhere else but Granby."[14] We want to be a *local* church because we want to live out the gospel within a small-town culture that values locality and community. We prefer to live *in* the circle rather than tearing it up. We've seen how the overlapping of relationships in our small town creates pathways along which the gospel can run.

I can pop into the grocery store in the center of Pepperell and immediately encounter several people I know. Recently, I was at the town library, speaking with a friend who works behind the desk, when our town planner, also a friend, walked in, followed soon after by a woman from our church with her grandson. We experience this overlap daily. The daughter of our dental hygienist lives up the street from us. The director of our local community youth theater goes to our church. The father of a boy in my son's Cub Scout troop is a local police officer who lives nearby. The woman who runs the AA meeting that meets at our church used to be the neighbor of good friends who attend our church.

We celebrate these overlaps and seek them out. Our family loves Saturday morning breakfasts at the diner in central

Pepperell, not only because the food is good but because we often see people we know from church, school, and neighborhood. Over the years I've made sure to be present in what sociologist Ray Oldenburg calls the "great good places" of our town: the public places where people congregate and socialize, like Dunkin' Donuts, the senior center, and the library.[15] Some small-town pastors emphasize the importance of being a regular—eating at the same restaurant, asking for the same server, going to the same checkout line. Getting my hair cut at a place on Main Street for many years has led to some amazing gospel conversations with my friends who work there. All this overlap creates opportunities for relationship and gospel witness.[16] It also makes it extra important to be kind to the worker at the post office, generous to the waiter who serves us, and peaceable toward our neighbors—because we don't have the luxury of anonymity. They'll see us again and will share what they know with others. Our church wants to opt into this circle. Churches and ministers who live outside the circle, who ignore their community, will also be ignored *by* their community.[17]

Our church is developing a regional vision, but it's not of the region driving to church in Pepperell. Rather, we long for every small town in our region to have its own gospel-centered church—one that lives happily within that town's circle of community, understanding its rhythms and routines. Our vision is "lots of churches close to people." For now, before that vision is a reality, we're happy to welcome those who don't have a healthy, gospel-preaching, community-engaged church in their own town. Our network of small groups allows them to meet nearer to their own neighborhoods and equips them to live on mission in their own towns. Perhaps one day they'll help us establish new churches (or revitalize existing ones) in their town. Of course, this vision may take a long time. It may mean that our church will be smaller than if we aimed to grow on-site by drawing people from across our region. But as the gospel (rather than the business world) permeates our thinking, we're increasingly okay with smaller and slower, even as we pray for God to amaze us with fast and big. If we had to choose, we'd rather be a small church that plants small churches than a large church that draws people in our region away from their local communities.

BE A LISTENING CHURCH

Being a local church means being a *listening* church. We need to study the people around us and understand what makes them tick. We should know how they speak and think, what they value, what they're proud of, what they like to eat, how they like to relax. Understanding Pepperell means knowing its history, its struggles, its hobbies, its cultural offerings, its businesses, its needs, its triumphs, and its aspirations.

Pepperell sent minutemen to fight the British in 1775. Pepperell native William Prescott was the commander of forces at the Battle of Bunker Hill and reportedly spoke the famous phrase, "Do not fire until you see the whites of their eyes." Pepperell people are proud of that. For years, Pepperell's paper mill (now closed) employed many in town, and that manufacturing culture has shaped our town's character. When I led the funeral of one of my neighbors several years ago, his former workmates at the mill attended. In more recent years, as Boston has expanded and high-tech industry around Boston has flourished, highly educated engineers and white-collar workers have come north looking for housing, land, and local communities with good schools. This has affected the character of our town and created some tensions. All these things are important for our church to know. Knowing them is an act of love.

How can small-place churches develop a culture of listening? It often begins with ministers listening to the people in their churches and adapting accordingly. I learned this the hard way early in my ministry. I came to my small-town church after years of serving in churches full of university students and professors. When I arrived, fresh from teaching at a seminary, I introduced some rigorous theology books for our small groups to study. Week after week, my group began our time together by listing and defining all the vocabulary words we didn't know! Eventually, I caught on and began introducing resources that were more approachable, though just as robust in terms of biblical truth.

There was a marked difference between the Cambridge-educated William Grimshaw and the "wild and uncultivated" citizens of uncivilized Haworth. But, wonderfully, Grimshaw *listened*. He used images from daily life and preached in the common speech of his day, far from the polished style he had been trained in. He called it his "market language" for preaching, and he used it because he loved his people, was listening to them, and wanted to communicate the gospel to them. John Newton said Grimshaw's earnestness commanded the attention of his congregation. But his language and clarity allowed them to understand him.[18]

Ron Klassen, the executive director of the Rural Home Missionary Association and a former small-town pastor, tells of the transformation that occurred in his own perspective and ministry as he began to listen to his people and live among them. He learned to hunt because that's what the men in his church did. He rode along with ranchers in their tractors and went along to cattle sales. He wrestled calves, making a fool of himself the first time but earning the respect of the eight seasoned cowboys who watched him fall flat on his face in manure. He found that the farmers he listened to became more interested in hearing him preach God's Word.[19]

This will look different for every small-town minister. I've often eaten lunch with men in my church on construction sites and in office cafeterias. The point is to listen and learn. Church leaders who model the value of listening create a church culture of listening.

In an effort to know our town, our church has created a series of forums in which local community leaders share their perspective on the needs of our town. We thank them for what they're doing and prayerfully consider how we can serve with them. This isn't complicated—any church can do it. Do you know the culture of your place? Do you know and love its "deep traditions" or are you seeking to transcend them? Is your church listening?[20]

BE A SERVING CHURCH

The gospel confronts the dark realities of small-town life such as the racism often found in small places and the prevalent sense of hopelessness and despair.[21] But it also affirms some small-place values. The overlapping relationships within the smaller circle of small places increase a sense of mutual responsibility. This means that in times of crisis, the community rallies. People look to each other, not just government agencies, for help.[22]

When a fire destroyed the home and possessions of a father and son in our town, the entire community sprang into action, providing food, gift certificates, and clothing. Our church was glad to participate—it would have been odd if we hadn't. One small-town pastor friend told of canceling their Sunday services after a tornado ripped through the middle of town so that members of his church could be among the first running chainsaws and clearing debris. Being a serving church doesn't require lots of resources, and it doesn't mean reinventing the wheel. Rather than creating new initiatives, it may be better to support things your town is already doing well. Our church hasn't opened a food pantry because our town already has an excellent one. We've focused on being as generous to it as we can, volunteering and making frequent donations.

Being a serving church happens both when the church is gathered as a group to help our community and when it is scattered to serve individually in everyday life. Several years ago we started a tradition called Service Sunday. On the Sunday after our town's Fourth of July parade, our church has an early worship service and then floods out into town in teams. We clean debris from the parade route and the town field (where the fireworks were held) and do yardwork for seniors and others who need help. Local residents in our community have noticed and appreciated this effort ("Oh, you're the church that . . ."). Service happens regularly within our small groups as well. They have served shut-ins, caroled at nursing homes, raked lawns, and served at soup kitchens and homeless shelters. The team service of the church gathered doesn't replace the service that happens when we scatter into everyday life. Rather, the joy we experience serving together fuels our everyday service. We want to be a church that's so invested in our small community that we'd be sorely missed if we disappeared tomorrow.

BE A CELEBRATING CHURCH

Celebrations are one of the most important identity shapers for small towns. In Pepperell, it's the annual Fourth of July parade and fireworks. A volunteer committee works hard all year to raise funds for the parade on Main Street and the fireworks on the town field. Local businesses, politicians, community groups, marching bands, Boy Scout and Girl Scout troops, and the Daughters of the American Revolution walk or ride in the parade. It's a big deal. People place lawn chairs along the street hours before the parade begins in order to save their spot. Most of the town is there. Several years ago our church began thinking more about what it meant to be part of our community. We wanted to be friends and supporters of our town. We were already serving the town, but we realized that friends don't *only* serve one another. Sometimes they simply enjoy time together. We saw the parade as a high point of our town's life, a time to have fun and celebrate, so we created a float and joined the parade. We don't pass out tracts. We do throw a lot of candy, and we see a lot of people we know along the parade route. We celebrate with our town because that's what friends do and because genuine friendships create pathways for the gospel.

Many small towns have a strong community spirit. The local school is often a source of great pride. So it makes sense for our church members to be heavily invested in the schools—teaching, volunteering, serving. Rhythms as simple as the daily drop-off and pickup of our kids have led to friendships in town and fruitful gospel conversations. To say thank you, our church has left donuts for the teachers. One woman in our church took an extra minute to encourage a school teacher at the end of a busy week— her simple kindness elicited tears from the teacher.

Many small towns particularly love sports, so why not encourage your church to be present and cheering at the high school football games? While the level of play at our kids' soccer games is far from stellar, the conversations with other parents have created and deepened friendships. When our town launched a local youth theater, our kids were in the production along with others from our church. On performance night, many church members came to cheer them on. My heart leaped as I looked out over the crowd and saw our church celebrating this event as part of our town.

BE A PROCLAIMING CHURCH

It's not enough to be a local, listening, serving, celebrating church. To be the church, we must proclaim the gospel that creates and shapes us. Some of us are tempted to undercontextualize the gospel in our place and culture. We may proclaim the gospel in ways that unnecessarily offend or confuse those around us. I've visited small-town churches that communicated using insider language and long-forgotten forms of speech and music that erected unnecessary barriers for visitors. Churches that run from or condemn the culture will benefit from seeking to grow in the ways I've already mentioned. If we're a local, listening, serving, and celebrating church, we'll have genuine friends in town, and they may actually be interested in the gospel words we speak.

On the other hand, some of us tend toward abandoning the gospel by overcontextualizing to our place and culture. We become syncretistic, blending in rather than standing out. When my friend in town asked about our church's views on sexuality, it was an opportunity to share gospel words—backing away from that conversation would have been a missed opportunity. Several years ago, when I noticed that the neighbor I've built a friendship with was in distress, offering to pray for her was important. The gospel pathways created by genuine friendships are there *for the gospel to travel along.* The gospel is news that must be verbally proclaimed, and the more we love it, the more we will speak it. The new believers who have come to Christ in our church have usually trusted in Jesus after being told about him by a friend. When William Grimshaw moved to Haworth, one of the first changes he made in the church building was installing a new pulpit, marking the priority of gospel proclamation. He had two verses carved above the pulpit. "I am determined to know nothing among you save Jesus Christ and him crucified" and "For to me to live is Christ and to die is gain."[23]

The impulse to undercontextualize the gospel leads us to lose touch with our culture, stepping outside the circle. The impulse to overcontextualize leads us to lose the gospel altogether. As we've seen, the Bible never calls us to love our place and hate God or to love God and hate our place. Instead, we're called to love both God and our place. We're called to live within the circle of our town, seeking to transform that circle through the gospel.

9

Battling Joy Killers
in Small-Place Ministry

G EORGE HERBERT was groomed for greatness. Born in 1593 into a wealthy, powerful family in Wales, he graduated with multiple degrees from the University of Cambridge. In 1620, at the age of twenty-seven, he was elected the University Orator of Cambridge (a post he had greatly desired). In that capacity he addressed King James, Prince Charles, and other famous and influential leaders of the day. It looked as though he was on his way to an important career in the court of the king.

But in 1630, at the age of thirty-six, Herbert made a surprising career move. He took holy orders in the Church of England and became the rector of St. Andrews Church in the rural village of Bemerton, a parish of fewer than two hundred people. By all accounts he was a holy, humble, and devoted pastor. But his ministry was a brief one: he had suffered from poor health for much of his life, and in 1633 he died of consumption, one month shy of his fortieth birthday. He left behind a wife and the three orphaned nieces who lived with them. He also left behind a collection of poems that would be published by a friend soon after his death. Those poems would ensure Herbert's lasting fame and his reputation as one of the great metaphysical poets.

It's important not to romanticize Herbert's choice or his subsequent ministry. While Bemerton was a small village, it was an easy walk to the cathedral city of Salisbury. (Herbert attended services in the cathedral a couple of times every week and played music afterward with the cathedral musicians.) While Herbert took a humble post, he remained well-connected. (Wilton House, the country seat of his cousins, the Earls of Pembroke, was also nearby.) Moreover, he had two other clergy to help him in his tiny parish. This wasn't exactly John Paton among the cannibals of the South Pacific.

For all that, it's worth asking why Herbert forsook the prestige of a successful academic and political career for a humble rural ministry. Some have suggested that the death of key political sponsors weakened his career prospects in the direction of the court, but that by itself surely doesn't explain the integrity and passion with which Herbert pursued his subsequent parish ministry.

I think there's a better clue to Herbert's choice in his poem "The Elixir." In it, Herbert uses the famous image of the philosopher's stone (an elemental substance thought in his day to be capable of transforming other substances) to describe the key to performing lowly tasks and serving lowly people with grace and joy. The secret (the elixir) is to see God in all things and to do all things for God.

> This is the famous stone
> That turneth all to gold:
> For that which God doth touch and own
> Cannot for less be told.

This elixir turned Bemerton to gold. Herbert saw that God himself touched and owned the village and the church. A small ministry there wasn't less or worse than a heady political career at court. In fact, it was an opportunity for joy.

JOY KILLERS IN SMALL PLACES

God's people everywhere are called to "rejoice always" and to delight themselves in the Lord. The apostle Paul described himself as working for the joy of those he served (2 Corinthians 1:24). But we all know this is sometimes difficult. It can certainly be hard for Christian ministers. Ministry anywhere is demanding: people make self-destructive choices, criticisms are leveled, apathetic congregants drift away, and angry congregants storm away. And certain joy killers are particularly powerful in small-place ministry. If small-place ministers are to be effective in working for the joy of others, we must be sure to guard and stoke our own. We must be aware of joy killers and diligently battle them. In this chapter we'll consider how to fight discontentment, envy, fear, and loneliness—for our joy and God's glory.

Discontentment. For some, the greatest joy killer in small-place ministry is the feeling that what you're doing doesn't count for much. The small place where you live is forgotten by the wider culture. The small church you serve is forgotten by the Christian culture. Perhaps your friends have gone on to higher-profile Christian work, and the importance of what they do is recognized by many. Does your ministry *matter*? Insecurity and discontentment are lurking at your door. The gospel is the best and only weapon for killing this joy killer.

The gospel goes to work on your discontentment in three ways. First, it declares God's love for you. You don't need to make something of your ministry in order to make something of yourself. God isn't waiting to see how you turn out. He's already chosen you as his own. You minister from God's total acceptance, not for it. Second, the gospel declares God's love for your place and church. This is George Herbert's elixir: God has "touched and owned" your small town. It matters to him—thus, the way we live, preach, and serve in our place is important. And third, small-place ministers have a unique opportunity to display aspects of God's character and God's gospel in ways not possible for a big church in a big place. If the success of any given church is its portrayal of God's wisdom, your small-town church can be a success not in spite of but *because of* its size.

One of George Herbert's earliest biographers, Izaak Walton, tells of a conversation Herbert had with a friend the night he was inducted into the Bemerton church as a priest. Herbert's words may be partially fabricated by Walton, but they chime so well with some of his poems that they likely represent his actual feelings.[1] Herbert reflected on his former political aspirations and his new job:

> I now look back on my aspiring thoughts, and think myself more happy than if I had attained what then I so ambitiously thirsted for; and I can now behold the Court with an impartial eye, and see plainly that it is made up of . . . pleasures that are so empty as not to satisfy when they are enjoyed. But in God and his service is a fulness of all joy and pleasure.[2]

Herbert would later write that a country pastor "holds the rule that nothing is little in God's service: if it once have the honour of [God's] name, it grows great instantly."[3]

The key to productive small-place ministry and a contented small-place minister is seeing that the place, the people in it, and the ministry among them *matter*. When we understand the importance of ministering to eternal souls, no matter how many or where they live, we won't think it trifling compared to larger, more public ministries. Instead, we'll tremble at its significance. Izaak Walton tells us that when Herbert was offered the tiny Bemerton parish, "the apprehension of the last great account that he was to make for the [care] of so many souls, made him fast and pray often, and consider for not less than a month; in which time he had some resolutions to decline . . . the priesthood."[4] He expressed this reluctance in his poem "The Priesthood" and had to be talked into accepting the post by the bishop. That little phrase "so many souls" is striking. Herbert was concerned there were *too many*, not too few.

If we see our places and people as God sees them, we'll see that our ministries matter, and once we're persuaded of that, we'll immerse ourselves in ministry with joy, even when it's tough, demanding, and invisible. We won't be on the lookout for a better, bigger position. We'll sink deeper into ours, seeing it as more than big enough. For Winn Collier's fictional small-town pastor Jonas McAnn, genuine love involves a steadfast commitment to a particular group of people living in a particular place. It requires loving them for who they are, not who he might wish them to become. McAnn writes to his congregation, "We do not need to be anything other than ourselves, people who bear God's image and God's love. . . . We do not need to live some other life in some other place."[5]

In fact, the committed friendship required by life, community, and ministry in a small place will *enlarge* the hearts of those willing to give and receive it.[6] It turns out that small places can be very good at promoting deep love. Rather than being distracted by discontentment, with wandering eyes toward bigger places, those who see that their places matter to God will look and look and look again at their place and people. They'll see clearly and delight greatly. This is love. You can't love a people you're trying to get away from.

Only one of the writings left behind by George Herbert at his death was in prose. It was called *The Country Parson, His Character, and Rule of Holy Life* and was first published in 1652—long after Herbert's death. It was Herbert's guide for rural ministry. As he says in the preface, it was written largely for himself as a mark to aim at in his vocation as a country minister. Throughout the book, Herbert urges country pastors to consider carefully their place and people, to "carry their eyes ever open, and fix them on their charge" rather than on professional advancement.[7] Herbert calls for country pastors to attend closely to the customs, habits, language, educational level, and particular sins and faults of their people. Because country people work hard for their living and therefore value money, ministers should avoid greed and luxury in their way of life. Because country people value integrity, ministers should always keep their word: "neither will they believe him in the pulpit whom they cannot trust in his conversation."[8] The country minister is to know the Bible and also his place. "He condescends even to the knowledge of tillage and pasturage, and makes great use of them in teaching, because people by what they understand are best led to what they understand not."[9]

Underlying Herbert's ministry manual is his conviction that there is dignity and value in rural ministry; while ministry in small places has plenty of difficulties, such a calling is worth a lifetime of care and devotion. For the rural pastor, his place and people are "all his joy and thought."[10] This is love. Herbert insisted that the distinguishing mark of a country pastor ought to be his love for others and that the great "business and aim" of the country pastor is to stir up love among the members of his flock. We'll only do that if we ourselves love our flock.

Envy. The second joy killer, envy, is closely related to discontentment. It's not a sin anyone likes to admit or discuss, but it's common and deadly. Some years ago I visited a dear friend in his famous city. We went to a late-night jam session in a bar, into boutique shops, great coffee places, and a famous cinema. We talked about his church and ministry plans. I could feel envy welling up in my heart. Of course, envy isn't unique to ministers in small places (I've heard city pastors confess their envy of other city pastors), but I suspect it's common among us. Envy of where others are and what others have can cripple us spiritually and lead us to squander the opportunities right in front of us. We desperately need to kill this joy killer.

Here are some strategies I've found helpful in my own battle against envy.[12] Wielding these weapons doesn't guarantee quick victory, but they will keep us in the thick of the fight.

> *See clearly.* We need to recognize envy for what it is: abominable pride. The Puritan Thomas Watson wrote, "A humble Christian is content to be laid aside if God has any other tools to work with which may bring him more glory."[11] This humility is the opposite of envy, which yearns to possess what others have. Envy is an expression of selfishness and pride. Years ago, I heard that a friend had been invited to speak at Harvard University and felt a flash of envy at his opportunity. Then I had an unexpected thought: Christ was proclaimed by this gospel-loving brother, and I got to spend the evening with my family! What a win for me. The name of Jesus was exalted. Who cares about the instrument?

> *Confess openly.* Several years ago, I looked a close friend in the eye and confessed my envy of his abilities and successes. I asked for his forgiveness. It was humbling and helpful. I'm not suggesting we confess to every single person we ever envy, but we should do so particularly when we begin to envy someone close to us; otherwise we're not serving them well as a faithful friend. Our confession will allow them to pray for us, and the act of naming the sin will help to minimize its power over us.

> *Pray instead.* When I pray for the success of someone I envy, my heart begins to change. Envy pits me against them, but prayer puts me on their team. I'm now calling God's blessing down upon them. I'm investing emotionally in their

well-being. I begin to envy them less. In fact, their further successes now become answers to my prayers. I *asked* God for the very thing they've now accomplished. How can I resent it?

Pursue friendship. Envy both isolates and feeds on isolation. It's difficult to grow a genuine friendship with those who trigger our sinful feelings of inadequacy, unhappiness, and discontentment. As a result, we may begin to avoid the people or situations that make us feel that way. Envy, in turn, thrives on that isolation. When we're not in genuine relationship with those we envy, we won't actually love and rejoice with them in their successes. Neither will we see their real struggles and insecurities. Instead, we'll spin our own distorted narrative and the complex realities and hardships of that other person's life won't even enter into it. It turns out one of the very best ways to kill envy is to cultivate friendship.

Identify idols. Over the years, God has helped me glimpse some of the root causes of my envy, and this has helped enormously. In spite of the unconditional love of godly parents, from an early age I forged a deep identification between identity and performance that has endured into my adult years. It's not difficult to see how envy thrived: if I'm valuable because of what I achieve, and someone else can do it better, they *are* better than me. Comprehending the roots of my own envy has helped me better understand its enduring power.

Run to the gospel. To combat the idols of my heart, I now fight envy more consciously by setting my heart and mind on gospel promises and regularly reminding myself (especially at the beginning of the day) of my identity in Jesus. Because this temptation will likely not disappear any time soon, I know I must *keep on* preaching the gospel to myself and hearing it from others.

Find small-place heroes. Our evangelical culture praises big-place ministers. Find small-place ministers and seek out examples of true greatness and success in small places. Pursue personal mentors you can speak with, and seek mentors you can read (and read about) from the past. I've been helped by studying the lives of William Grimshaw, John Berridge, George Herbert, and others. I've been encouraged by fictional portrayals of small-town ministers like John Ames in Marilynne Robinson's novel *Gilead*.

Remember judgment day. Perhaps you've heard the famous quote from John Brown of Haddington. In a letter to one of his newly ordained pupils who was pastoring a small congregation, he said,

I know the vanity of your heart, and that you will feel mortified that your congregation is very small, in comparison with those of your brethren around you; but assure yourself on the word of an old man, that when you come to give an account of them to the Lord Christ, at his judgment-seat, you will think you have had enough.[13]

We can be very thankful that God knows exactly where to place us in ministry and has done so for our joy and his glory.

Fear. Fear is a joy killer and ministry crippler for any gospel minister, but there are several ways it may get a particular purchase in the hearts of those in small places.

Financial fears. Anxiety about finances can be a joy killer in ministry. In small country churches, it can feel like we're constantly struggling to survive. Will we be able to pay the bills and keep the doors open? Some small-place churches teeter on the edge of being able to pay their pastor. Will it be necessary to pick up part-time work?

People fears. No matter where you minister, fearing people is a temptation. But when you're in a small place, particular aspects of this fear may be heightened. If your congregation is tiny, you may feel that you can't afford to lose members by offending them. It's also the case that rural and small-town churches not uncommonly have multiple generations of families attending. This creates an opportunity to serve people: I've found that time invested in children and grandchildren is also a major encouragement to their parents and grandparents. But it can also create fear on the part of ministers because families in small churches are sometimes powerful ruling clans. Some of the people who have become the most upset with me were angry because they felt I wronged their children. Fear of offending entire families (who may constitute a sizable percentage of the entire congregation) may incline us to avoid necessary ministry and difficult conversations.

Failure fears. Even city pastors with large churches can get discouraged when "only" fifteen hundred people show up on a particular Sunday. But when you have seventy-five regular attenders (or 175) and a bunch are missing, you really feel it. It can create a fear of failure: the fear that your church may fail for lack of people or the fear that you've *already* failed because so few come to your church. I'm sad to say that over the years Sunday morning attendance has had too great a hold on my heart, my self-image, and my mood. I remember one particular Sunday morning when I was expecting a good crowd, it turned out many people were traveling and attendance was particularly low. After the service I felt shaken and discouraged. I wondered if the church would survive.

Where do these fears come from, and what gives them power? The fear that our small church will fail is fueled by our human tendency to seek comfort and security in visible numbers and strength. That's what spurred King David to take a census of his fighting men (1 Chronicles 21), and it's what led God to reduce Gideon's troops (Judges 7). Nobody *enjoys* weakness. If big-church ministers aren't careful, their efforts to grow their churches will in fact be attempts to "flee vulnerability through size."[14] If small-church ministers aren't careful, they'll live in perpetual fear. We all need to be reminded of the Bible's teaching that military might can't save the day: "The war horse is a false hope for salvation, / and by its great might it cannot rescue" (Psalm 33:17). There's a better way to live: "Some trust in chariots and some in horses, / but we trust in the name of the LORD our God" (Psalm 20:7). We're gospel people. We've seen God's love for us at the cross, so we know he'll provide for us in our vulnerability and weakness and will forgive us when we trust in ourselves, our attendance, and our budget. We also know through the gospel the peculiar benefits of being small and weak. The gospel provides us assurance of God's help, forgiveness in failure, and a vision for fruitful ministry.

After that one particular Sunday of low attendance, I realized that something was askew in my soul and repentance was in order. I began reading a book I'd received as a gift months earlier. *Memoirs of an Ordinary Pastor* is Don Carson's biography of his father Tom Carson, an unheralded, twentieth century, Canadian pastor who served in ministry for nearly six decades. Tom was never famous. But he read widely, ministered deeply, cared for his wife, shepherded his children, studied the biblical languages, memorized Scripture, and had a vibrant experience of God and the gospel until the day he died. He knew the joy of Christ in the midst of suffering. As I read about Tom Carson's life, God stirred in me a desire for integrity in my own life and ministry, and a passion to do well what I do, whether or not it's known by others. God has produced good fruit since then. I still fight fears when we miss our monthly budget or I see more empty seats than expected, but I know where to turn with my fears.

Loneliness. Ministry in small places can be lonely. You may not live in close proximity to other ministers. If your town is remote and your church has a tiny budget, there may be no funds to travel to a big conference in a big place. Sometimes you may feel like you're on the margins, forgotten and alone. That's a joy killer.

Throughout my years of ministry, I've come increasingly to see the importance of meeting regularly with other ministers for encouragement, support, discussion, accountability, and wisdom. I need wise friends in ministry. It's worth driving miles to sustain these friendships. The two small groups of ministers I belong to pray for me and sharpen me theologically. I trust them to speak at my church and to help me with thorny pastoral problems. Meeting in person is best, but technology also allows us to connect with ministry friends around the globe. More recently, I've joined a group of small-town pastors who meet monthly online to discuss the particular opportunities and challenges of our ministry contexts.

The importance of gospel partnership in small places led me to start a group some years ago with a couple of friends called Small Town Summits. We knew there were many ministers and churches scattered throughout our region of New England, most of them in small places outside the few big cities. We began to ask how we could encourage and support them. While we appreciate and participate in the big conferences in the big cities with well-known speakers, they aren't usually geared for small places. What we learn can be hard to translate back into our own contexts. So we've launched a series of small summits (often with fifty to eighty attendees all told, including pastors, laypeople, and ministry leaders), each focused on a particular state or region. We call them summits because in common parlance a summit is a gathering of leaders who discuss important issues for the sake of taking action. We believe there's great value in hearing and learning from faithful pastors, ministry leaders, and Christian workers already engaged in small-place ministry. Because our Small Town Summits are small, they're collaborative, contextual (we meet in small churches in small towns), affordable, and reproducible. Because they're local to a state or region, there's an opportunity for gospel partnerships after they're over.

We've found that small-place pastors and lay leaders are grateful for these gatherings. One said, "What an answer to prayer. It's like a cold drink of water in the desert." Others have told us that the very existence of a conference devoted to their ministry context is an encouragement. We're not doing anything particularly brilliant. Our model can easily be reproduced beyond our own region of New England.

The reality is that, while ministry in any place can be lonely at times, and while God may choose to call us to periods of loneliness, small-place ministers don't need to resign ourselves to inevitable, perpetual loneliness. We can find ways to engage with one another and help each other in the work of ministry.

A SMALL-PLACE PRAYER

George Herbert is commemorated in the Anglican Communion every year on February 27. One of the collects for that day, based on Herbert's poem "The Elixir," has been hanging in my study for years. Early most Sunday mornings, I close my time of sermon preparation by praying the words of the collect. If you're a pastor who longs to see the eternal significance of what you do, I invite you to pray these words with me and thousands of others:

> Our God and King, who called your servant George Herbert from the pursuit of worldly honors to be a pastor of souls, a poet, and a priest in your temple: Give unto us the grace, we

pray, joyfully to perform the tasks you give us to do, knowing that nothing is menial or common that is done for your sake; through Jesus Christ our Lord, who lives and reigns with you and the Holy Spirit, one God, for ever and ever. Amen.

PART 3

SHOULD I BE MINISTERING IN A SMALL PLACE?

(Reasons Not to Do Small-Place Ministry, Reasons You Should, and Reasons to Consider)

(10)

Good and Bad Reasons
Not to Do Small-Place Ministry

I N THIS BOOK I've developed a theological vision for ministry in small places. We've seen that small towns and rural areas are simultaneously better and worse than we usually think and that God desires his church to be present and available in every place, no matter its size or influence, displaying the wonders of his character in a thousand ways. The very shape of the gospel sends God's people to places big and small, fast and slow, powerful and weak—and equips them with resources for ministry once they get there.

Because God means for his church to be present in small places, it's clear he calls his people to minister there. But here's a much more specific question, one this final section is intended to help you prayerfully consider: Should *I* be ministering in a small place?

This question applies to those already ministering in forgotten places. One small-town pastor told me, "I really want to be faithful where I am and not see it as 'less than.'" Another friend transitioned from leading a dynamic university student ministry in an influential church in a big city to pastoring a small church in another part of the city, an area with vacant lots, low incomes, and little influence. He soon noticed a corresponding decrease in his own influence—now that he had moved away from the center of things, he received fewer requests from ministry colleagues for meetings. Yet another friend has pastored a tiny church in a remote town of four thousand for fifteen years. Each week he types the bulletin, prepares the slides for music, and tends to other small matters at church. "I wrestle with significance," he writes, "and wondering if it really matters and couldn't I be having a much greater impact somewhere else. People continue to leave [my town]. Students graduate and don't come back. We have one older pianist and no other musicians." All these people are wrestling with the same underlying question: Should I be ministering in a small place?

I've written this book for faithful ministers like these three friends. In this final section I want to help them (and you) address the question of whether to remain in place. My prayer is that if you're already a small-place minister, you won't stay where you are simply because it's easier, safer, and more convenient to do so—because you have a secure salary and decent housing you don't care to lose or because you're too afraid of moving elsewhere to do what you feel God may be calling you to do. I pray also that you won't *leave* your current ministry because you hear the siren song of making a name for yourself in a famous, important place. Neither inertia's tug nor ambition's pull lead to the confident joy and kingdom effectiveness of God's call. Whether you stay in your small place or leave it, I pray it will be because you're persuaded it's what God wants.

The question, Should I be ministering in a small place? applies also to those who aren't currently in a small place but who dare to ask whether God wants them to give their lives to one. As we'll see, there are excellent reasons *not* to live and minister in a small place. God sends his servants all over the world, to great cities, medium-sized suburbs and exurbs, and tiny, no-name villages and townships. He may choose to send you to a big or medium-sized place. Wendell Berry once said, "Not all ministers should be country ministers, just as not all people should be country people."[1] I think he's right.

But here's the key: every one of us ought to be open to whatever God is calling us to do, wherever he's calling us to do it. When the God of Israel asked, "Whom shall I send, and who will go for us?" the trembling prophet Isaiah replied, "Here I am! Send me" (Isaiah 6:8). He didn't qualify his availability ("Send me to people who are like me . . . to educated professionals . . . to influencers who will influence others"). In fact, God gave Isaiah a ministry he certainly wouldn't have chosen for himself: a ministry of judgment.

Bible college or seminary student, layperson, minister: can you say without qualification, "Here I am! Send me"? Are you willing for God to surprise you? Or have you already taken some options off the table? That's not uncommon for Christians to do. Researchers have found that the evangelical church in past generations bought into (and even strengthened) a prevailing American anti-urban bias. As a result, evangelicals have tended to gravitate toward the suburbs.[2] But more recently, some sectors of evangelicalism have decisively shifted to a *pro*-urban leaning.

Either one can deafen us to God's call. As a seminary student, I wasn't open to God's call to small. I wouldn't have heard even if he asked. Surveys show that most prospective pastors take community size and growth potential seriously in weighing where they'll go.[3] Of course, that's fine as one factor among others. But it's a problem when it's our main or only factor. If you rule out small churches in small places in advance, you may miss God's call.

DISCERNING GOD'S CALL

How do we discern God's call? In some cases his will for our lives is clearly evident. For instance, we know that personal holiness and pervasive thankfulness are God's will for every Christian because he tells us so in the Bible (1 Thessalonians 4:3; 5:18). But of course the Bible doesn't specifically tell us where God wants us to live and minister. In making such decisions, we have to weigh a range of factors, including our natural aptitudes and spiritual giftings, our opportunities and circumstances, and our desires and inclinations. We have to discern how God is prompting us through his Holy Spirit (perhaps through an inner sense or through a dream), to take into account what is wise and foolish and to welcome the guidance of godly people, all while carefully evaluating our own motives. The apostle Paul was flexible in his missionary strategy. He didn't expect to travel to Macedonia, but when God called him through a vision to preach the gospel there, he obeyed (Acts 16:6-10).

We don't need to be paralyzed, afraid that we'll ruin our lives if we miss God's call. Instead, we can seek to make wise decisions while trusting the sovereign God to provide for us no matter what. Let's consider some good reasons—and some bad ones—*not* to go to (or remain in) a small place.

SOME GOOD REASONS NOT TO MINISTER IN SMALL PLACES (WHY WE SHOULDN'T GO)

The best reason not to minister in a small place is that God has called you to a big or medium-sized one. God is calling many choice servants to the great cities of the world because of the tremendous spiritual needs there. By 2050, more than twenty-five cities will have populations of more than 16 million people, and, according to Allan Barth, the vice president of Redeemer City to City, of the five cities with more than 40 million residents (Lagos, Karachi, Bombay, Dhaka, and Calcutta), four will likely be hostile to Christianity.[4] It's no wonder God is sending servants to cities. Years ago, God led one of my best friends to plant a church in a major city. The call came as he prayed, read, talked with others, and traveled there. The desire to go became overwhelming, and the fruit of his ministry has been abundant. Of course, it's not just planters and pastors who God calls to the city. It's breathtaking to hear of churches such as Bethlehem Baptist Church in Minneapolis or The Stone in Austin, where numerous families have moved into difficult city neighborhoods in order to learn from and love those around them.

It may be that God has burdened and gifted you to reach a particular segment of the population. As Stephen Um and Justin Buzzard note, cities are magnets for the *aspirational* (those who want to make a name for themselves), the *marginalized* (those who don't fit neatly into the larger society), and the *explorational* (free spirits in search of new experiences or a fresh start). Because cities are the homes of universities, technology companies, research hospitals, and other important cultural institutions, they attract a disproportionate number of young, ambitious people.[5] Because cities attract dense human populations, those who live on the margins of society or simply don't conform to middle-class norms are drawn to find others like them.[6] Singles and artists tend to gather in cities. Because new things are always happening, those who want to explore and start afresh come. Cities provide more social services for those in need and therefore are places of refuge for minorities or immigrants. Of course, you'll find immigrants, artists, singles, young people, university students, minorities, and the homeless living in small places but not to the same extent. If God has gifted and burdened you to minister to these groups—or to government workers, artists, film producers, or professionals—he may be calling you to the city.

It may be that God has arranged the circumstances of your life in a way that makes clear he wants you in a city or suburb. Perhaps you grew up in a city, and it's your native environment, affording you a tremendous advantage in navigating urban life and ministry. Maybe you attended a city university and God opened academic or professional doors, making it clear you're to remain there. Maybe you never specifically aimed to minister in a city, but God led you to a church that happened to be in one. Or maybe you moved to a city in order to prioritize your family, honoring your spouse by moving closer to parents or serving your unwell child by getting nearer to extra medical care.

These are all potentially good reasons to minister in a big place rather than a small one. I'm thankful that Martyn Lloyd-Jones, after ministering for a decade in Aberavon, Wales, obeyed God's call to move to Westminster Chapel in London. I'm thankful that Tim Keller obeyed God's call to plant Redeemer Presbyterian Church in Manhattan after nine years of ministry in Hopewell, Virginia. If God calls us to minister in a big place (at least for a season of our lives), we shouldn't be in a small one.

SOME BAD REASONS NOT TO MINISTER IN SMALL PLACES (WHY WE DON'T GO)

Though it's unlikely anyone would state the following reasons explicitly, they're common. And even if they don't prevent us from ministering in a small place, they may keep us from doing so joyfully and fruitfully.

There are no good coffee shops and few cultural opportunities. I'd find it too boring. Over the years I've attended shows in Prague, Chicago, and the West End of London. I've enjoyed the museums, shops, cafes, and monuments of Barcelona, Rome, Berlin, Hong Kong, Paris, and other great world cities. My small town simply can't compete. We have more pizza places than performing arts centers, more nail salons than live music venues, and more gas stations than museums. Of course, many residents of small places don't particularly mind (perhaps that's why they live where they do), but others miss the intoxicating energy of the city.[7] Some would-be ministers simply don't want to make that sacrifice: "Young evangelicals are not motivated to go to places that are not very desirable places to live."[8] That quote is both clearly true and deeply troubling. Good coffee and live music are gifts from God to be enjoyed, but it's a shameful tragedy if their absence is enough to keep God's people from going to a small place. That's not the radical gospel sacrifice that took the good news to Africa and Asia. Tim Keller warns against thinking of the city as an "adult playground," a place to be entertained and amused. The presence or absence of cultural opportunities should never be a determining factor in where we minister.

I'm too gifted/educated for a small place. Will your degree be wasted in a place full of people who don't have one? Will your gifts be lost on a tiny church that needs you to visit the elderly, teach a children's class, prepare the bulletin, and answer the office phones? Absolutely not—if God has called you there. No human being is overqualified to minister to other human beings. When God sends a choice servant to a small charge, he's not squandering resources—he's demonstrating his love. Do we doubt that God in his sovereign wisdom can give a big talent a small platform? That he can send Jonathan Edwards to the edge of the wilderness in Stockbridge, Massachusetts; William Grimshaw to uncouth Haworth; and George Herbert to tiny Bemerton? We should remind ourselves that he sent his Son Jesus to spend lots of time in Nazareth, Capernaum, and other tiny villages.

Those who walk closely with God and are deeply engaged in small-place ministry soon realize they're not overqualified to stand before God's people and declare the mysteries of the gospel. They're not overqualified to help a couple whose marriage is dangling by a thread or to share the gospel with a neighbor. In those moments we don't cherish our diplomas or wish for a greater challenge; we cling to God with desperate prayers.

Maybe you've recently received a seminary degree and can't imagine moving to a tiny town where few people have graduated from college. Maybe you think you'd be more effective in ministry to people who are close to your age, share your cultural reference points, and possess your level of education and intellectual curiosity. While understandable, this view needs to be challenged. The apostle Paul didn't look for people who were like him; he found people and sought to make himself like *them* for the sake of the gospel. Consider Darren Carlson's piercing question: "Most of the Reformed ministry with which I'm familiar aims for fellow thinkers. We love reaching young, educated, globally minded, influential people who live in diverse cities. So who will reach the lower ends of the middle class?"[9] Eugene Peterson writes of the period in his ministry when he discovered that "in the cultural flatland of suburbia the people to whom I was pastor had no interest in books or the life of the mind." This was a hardship. But he realized God had given him responsibility for *souls*, even though his people were unlike him.[10]

I want to make a name for myself, and the city is the best place to do that. Boris Johnson, the erstwhile mayor of London and former British Foreign Secretary, once admitted that "above all, talented people seek cities for fame. They can't get famous in the [expletive] village. . . . That's what's driving me. That's the awful fact."[11] Cities attract ambitious people. While they swallow far more of those ambitious people into anonymity than they elevate to fame, it's also a fact that the best-known Christian leaders live and minister in cities. J. C. Ryle once reflected on why William Grimshaw wasn't better known. He concluded it was because of his location.

> Within that orbit, no doubt, he was a star of the first magnitude; but beyond it he was never heard or seen. We need not wonder that he was little known in his day and generation. The minister who never preaches in London, and writes nothing, must not be surprised if the world knows nothing of him.[12]

There are times when walking through some great city I'll see a magnificent church building with its spire soaring upward. I'll wonder what it would feel like to see my name engraved on the sign, and the potential of prestige will send a tingle up my spine. That's an indication of the idol of prestige in my life and a reminder that I desperately need the gospel. Living in a small place certainly isn't a remedy for my pride, but it's good for my soul that I gain no points when I tell people I'm from Pepperell (and then need to spell it and explain where it is). Boston or London might offer a measure of greatness by association, but my pride doesn't need to be boosted. It needs to be battered.

My father-in-law served as a pastor in Northern Ireland for more than thirty years. During his first pastorate, the small church that called him grew significantly, adding services and staff and attracting a dynamic city congregation with lots of professionals. This was great for the gospel. But as he was drawn into leading the staff and keeping a large church running, he found himself less involved in the pastoral duties he most loved. Eventually, he made an unusual career decision. He sought a smaller church farther from the city and embraced the tasks of preaching, praying, and visitation within a small congregation. That may not be your career path, but none of us should allow pride to prevent us from such downward mobility. The smallness of a place may (or may not) be a reason to go there, but it should never be a reason *not* to go there.

Small-place ministry is too difficult. Small-place ministers work hard, often for low pay and little recognition. Their ministries can be lonely, draining, humble, and discouraging, with few visibly impressive results. Some of their churches can't afford a full salary, requiring them to be bivocational (whether or not that's their preference). But difficulty isn't a good reason not to do something. God frequently calls his people to do hard things and then equips them beyond their own means to do them.

Besides, those who eschew small-place ministry because it's too difficult will find city ministry no easier. Church planting in cities has been romanticized in recent years in ways that have

surprised even leaders of the movement.[13] John Starke, a pastor
in Manhattan, warns of what he calls the "enchantment of the
city," the intoxication of being associated with urban elites. In
contrast, Starke writes that

> what should be communicated to church planters is just
> how unattractive, humiliating, confusing, tiring, and lonely
> long-term church planting, revitalizing, and pastoring is,
> especially in the city. I talk to more homeless neighbors than
> "cultural elites." I spend more time calling and waiting for
> paramedics to help unconscious folks on our front steps
> than I do giving talks at the Googleplex.[14]

The high cost of city living can lead to debt, and the transience of
the city can lead to discouragement as treasured friends and colleagues regularly move away.

Ministry will be difficult in both big and little places. That
needn't prevent us from doing it. Thankfully, we have a God who
promises to be with us wherever we go (Matthew 28:18-20).

WHAT I WOULD SAY TO MY FORMER SEMINARY SELF

I said earlier in this chapter that when I graduated from seminary,
I wouldn't have seriously considered a call to a small place. It
wasn't on my list of options. If I could now go back to my former
seminary self, here's what I'd like to say:

> Please think very big about things that are truly big: God's
> character, God's gospel, God's mercy, God's glory. Know, and
> firmly believe, and often remind yourself that these truly
> big things do not depend on the size of your place, your
> church, your ministry, or your reputation. Focus on your
> ministry's depth. Let God tend to its breadth. Remember
> that when we think too big in terms of ourselves or our
> place, we're limiting how God may be pleased to surprise

and use us—which means we're not thinking big enough. So, think bigger than big. As you consider what comes next after seminary, don't limit yourself to big places. Put all the options on the table. Open yourself to the leading of your big God, and go joyfully wherever he calls you.

11

Good and Bad Reasons to Do Small-Place Ministry

W E'VE CONSIDERED good and bad reasons not to do small-place ministry. Now let's consider some good and bad reasons *to* do it. Just as God calls some to sprawling suburbs and great cities, he calls others to the small places, and his call to small comes in a delightful variety of ways.

SOME GOOD REASONS TO MINISTER IN A SMALL PLACE (WHY WE SHOULD GO)

Perhaps your call to a small place begins when you honor your spouse by moving nearer to in-laws who live in a rural area; to your surprise, God allows you to both serve your family and discover a fruitful ministry. Maybe poor health requires you to live in the countryside, away from pollution and noise. Or maybe one day you leave the city looking for property you can afford (lots of people in my town tell me that's why they live here). However exactly you get to the country, once you settle down, you pursue everyday life with gospel intentionality because that's what God's people are all called to do. These are just a few of the ways God may call you to small-place ministry. Let's consider several others.

Your heart was formed in a small place. Perhaps you grew up in a rural, remote area and are well-suited to understand the rhythms and routines of small places. You're not fazed by what's lacking or frustrated by what's different. Sociologists confirm what we might have guessed ourselves: it's harder for urban people to grasp small-town values and assimilate to life in small places.[1] Donnie Griggs writes,

> I think indigenous missionaries are best for small towns. You can parachute into a place, but it's hard and takes considerable time to learn the context and earn trust. But if you're "from here," you start off knowing the people and the place. You speak the language. You understand the brokenness.[2]

Growing up in Monson was as important preparation for ministry in Pepperell as my years of graduate study. Biblical studies helped me understand and love my Bible, but the years I spent in rural Maine prepared me to understand and love my congregation.

Your heart falls for a small-place church. Even if you don't particularly like rural areas, God may cause you to fall in love with a church in one. Ron Klassen tells of graduating from seminary and traveling to Brewster, Nebraska, to candidate for an open pastoral position in the tiny church there. Klassen was from a big city. Brewster had twenty-one residents. The church was eleven miles outside of town. The last mile was a single lane, sand road, followed by a river crossing that consisted of a tiny bridge with no guardrails. He was certain that he'd tell the church he wasn't interested. But before leaving the town that weekend, God "arranged for us to fall deeply in love with these people. We said yes."[3]

My story is similar. I didn't choose a small town—instead, one was given to me.[4] After completing a PhD in New Testament studies, I taught at a university and a seminary while applying for a pastoral position. Finally, two churches expressed interest. One was in a wealthy suburb close to the city, with professionals and university students in the congregation and important people in leadership. It seemed like the obvious career move. The other church was in Pepperell. It was smaller and farther from the city. There were no Fortune 500 CEOs. Most of the college-aged kids had left for other places. On paper, it wasn't as appealing.

We sought God's leading every way we knew how, and a surprising thing happened. God strongly inclined us toward Pepperell Christian Fellowship. We were drawn to the biblical passion and pastoral integrity of the leadership team. We liked the people. We sensed a hunger for God's Word and saw a need for loving leadership. So we pulled out of the other search process. The counterintuitive movement toward what seemed weaker, smaller, and less impressive strangely appealed to me. It was less my natural preference and more like the way I saw God often working in the Bible.

Meanwhile, the eight members of the pastoral search committee in Pepperell had narrowed their field to two candidates. For a variety of good reasons, some members were looking for a seasoned leader to guide the congregation, so they supported the candidate with more years of experience. Others felt I'd be a good fit. After much discussion, the committee voted. The result was disconcerting: 4-4. They sought wisdom from the church elders, who told them to pray rather than discussing the matter further. During the following week, several members of the committee had unmistakable impressions of God's specific guidance. One told me (much later) that as he was working at his desk one day, he felt God's clear direction to call me as the next pastor. When the search committee met a week later the four who had voted to call Stephen Witmer were even more certain that this was God's will. The four who had voted otherwise had each (without discussing it among themselves) experienced a clear prompting to change their vote. That second vote was 8-0 to call me.

This is a humble, humbling, and encouraging story to tell. It's a humble story because it's about the calling of a no-name, normal pastor to a no-name, normal church. It's humbling because I didn't become a pastor by overwhelming the people of my church with my skill or charisma. But these events have been remarkably encouraging for me as I've learned about them (in pieces, a little at a time, over the past decade). God knew it would require a crystal-clear call to grab my attention and move me in an unexpected direction, rewriting the story I had planned for myself. In notes I jotted after accepting the church's offer to visit as their candidate for the position, I expressed *surprise*. I didn't pursue ministry in a small place because I loved small places. Just the opposite: I've come to a renewed love of small places through living and ministering in one.

Your heart beats for small places. My father grew up in busy, prosperous, fast-growing Lancaster County, Pennsylvania, but always felt drawn toward remote places. As a young man he spent time in Alberta, Canada, and loved the cold and snow. When he married my mother in 1973, they honeymooned in Maine and Canada. A couple of years later they moved to rural Maine, where my dad became the pastor of a three-church parish (each church too small to call its own full-time pastor). Over the course of more than four decades of life and ministry in Monson, my dad has invested deeply in his small congregation and our small town, serving as town moderator, planning the celebrations for the town's 175th anniversary, and caring for the people. My mom worked in the post office and knows almost every Monson resident. They've both had eyes to see the significance of what they're doing and hearts to love the people and the place.

If your heart beats faster when you think of small places—or perhaps one small place in particular that you've grown to love—that may be a good reason to follow your heart and to love deeply what God loves perfectly.

Your heart breaks for small places. It may be that you're not particularly attracted to living in a small place (maybe you'd prefer *not* to live in one), but your heart breaks for the tremendous needs there. Donnie Griggs grew up in small-town Morehead City, North Carolina, and left in 1999, moving to Texas and then California. He aimed to be a church planter and missionary, and he considered locations around the world—anywhere but his hometown. Then in 2008, while serving at a youth conference in North Carolina, he was confronted with the lack of spiritual growth in many of his high school friends, the surge of opioid use in small North Carolina towns, and the increasing suicide rate (some of his own high school friends had committed suicide). God broke his heart as he confronted the needs of his home region. Within months he and his wife moved across the country back to his hometown and started a church in their living room with childhood friends. Today, One Harbor Church is planting new sites, seeing people come to Christ, and deeply engaged in meeting the needs of Morehead City and other small towns on the North Carolina coast.

Some may question just how serious the *spiritual* needs of small places actually are. Aren't there already an inordinate number of church-going Christians in rural areas? This view is common, but it needs to be reexamined. With some exceptions (particularly the Bible Belt), rural areas usually match or exceed the national average of adults unaffiliated with any church (34 percent).[5] And while rural communities often value their local church, that doesn't mean rural people regularly *attend* it. In fact, only 36 percent do, not much higher than the national average.[6] Research shows that the lowest earners in the United States are in fact significantly *less* religious than the highest earners and that while many in the working class identify as Christians, they're actually "functionally secular."[7] Rural America is neither fully evangelized nor overchurched.

When we dig deeper than our preconceptions, we also find an urgent need for pastors in small places. In a study for Duke Divinity School, sociologist Patricia Chang found that "the congregations most vulnerable to pastoral vacancies are smaller or rural congregations, which lack the financial resources to attract and retain full-time ordained clergy."[8] A 2009 *Time* article noted that less than half of rural US churches have a full-time, seminary-educated pastor and that in some parts of the Midwest, only one in five churches do.[9] Village Missions, which supports and equips pastors in rural communities, reports that its greatest challenge is "not in finding churches asking for assistance but in recruiting students from Bible colleges and seminaries who are willing to serve in rural areas."[10] And Glenn Daman concludes that "the greatest challenge for rural churches in the future will be the recruitment and retention of pastors to serve their local congregation."[11]

Rural areas don't just need churches but *healthy* churches centered on the gospel and willing to engage with their communities. That's exactly what's missing in many small places. One Christian youth worker in a rural region reports that in the course of expanding ministry from fifteen to one hundred schools, he's never encountered opposition from *outside* the church but only from churches that oppose any engagement with the culture. One of his biggest challenges is finding healthy local churches for the kids being reached in the schools. After years at a nearby church with an undereducated pastor and an unhealthy internal culture, my friend now drives more than an hour to a big city so that his family can attend a healthy church with sound teaching.

But still, aren't there more churches per person in rural areas? Some have argued for prioritization of urban ministry based on the higher populations of cities and the greater number of churches per capita in nonurban areas. For instance, Tim Keller writes, "Even mathematically, it is obvious that cities are woefully underserved by the church," noting that most denominations have many more churches serving the combined 15 million people who live in Georgia and South Carolina than the 18-19 million people in the New York City metro area.[12]

While I agree that we need more Christians ministering in the big places, I wonder whether per capita thinking (in which we tally total populations and divide by the number of churches) may obscure the reality that people live not as individual demographic units but in *communities*. There are lots of *small* communities: "In sheer numbers, small nonurban towns of no more than 25,000 residents comprise 75 percent of all towns and cities nationally," which means that throughout America, on average, you'll come across a town of less than twenty-five thousand people every twelve miles.[13] Because small towns are scattered geographically, and because local community and relationships matter a great deal to small-town residents, it's important, for the sake of evangelism and discipleship, to have a healthy church in every small town and village—even the tiny ones. Friends of mine have planted churches in tiny towns because they discovered that people there were driving one and a half hours *one way* to a church whose theology and culture they loved. That's a great reason to plant a small-town church, even if it remains small forever.

Consider this analogy: in the United Kingdom, only about 20 percent of the population lives in rural areas, but about half of UK post offices are located in rural areas. Is that a disproportionate allocation? It is if you're only counting noses. But all those noses live in communities, which means there's a good case to be made for keeping the rural post offices. Rural populations are thinly spread (which means you have to drive further if your local post office closes), and in addition, closing a post office and a shop can badly damage the morale of a little village.[14] If we consider people in terms of the *communities* where they live, not simply in terms of the total population, we may not agree that there are an inordinate number of small-place churches. It may be that rural areas actually require more churches per capita than urban ones.

SOME BAD REASONS TO MINISTER IN A SMALL PLACE

I'll never forget visiting friends who were training indigenous pastors and serving orphans in northern Uganda. I was given the task of processing several large boxes of books that had been shipped from American donors to the mission's theological library. For two stiflingly hot days my missionary friend and I sorted through books. What we found was simultaneously funny and discouraging. There were a few valuable additions to the library, but the rest of the boxes were filled with a set of 1960s encyclopedias, car and computer manuals, random novels, and books of wacky theology and end-time speculation. It was the oddest assortment of cast-off books you could imagine. The donors had found a convenient way of getting rid of books they no longer wanted while feeling that they had benefited humanity.

As my friend and I spoke of his experience on the mission field, I began to think of the boxes of books as a metaphor. The American church sometimes sends its very best to the mission field: skilled, sensitive, wise, godly, highly trained, humble servants. But it also sends those who are too irresponsible, spiritually immature, bullheaded, or socially awkward to find church work at home. Not sure what to do with these folks, the church sends them overseas.

Or maybe they find their way instead to a small church in a small town. Some ministers retreat to a small place out of fear, laziness, or the feeling that they won't make it in a big place. This leads to mediocre ministries that don't engage with or learn from others. Kathleen Norris describes the dangers of slipping professional standards for teachers, doctors, lawyers, and ministers in rural areas: it's possible to get to a point where people don't just accept but actually *praise* what is mediocre "and refuse to see any outside standards as valid."[15] This attitude is an abdication of our responsibility. I've seen it almost kill a rural church.

Besides, pastors who go to small places because they feel they can get away with less intellectual rigor or dodge tough topics are setting themselves up for failure. Years of small-town ministry have taught me that just about every problem, struggle, and challenge imaginable will eventually manifest itself in my town and congregation. I need to be informed of the broader cultural trends of the day and prepared to help people think clearly, biblically, and wisely. There may be lower educational attainment in your congregation if you're in a remote rural town rather than a university setting, but education doesn't equal intelligence, nor does it merit a higher standard of pastoral care.

The urgent needs of rural places require ministers with deep wisdom, clear thinking, strong vision, unflagging energy, and tenacious perseverance. We need some of God's choicest servants in small places. Such places should never be treated as dumping grounds or training grounds for those unfit or unready for ministry. It's certainly not wrong to start in a small place and move to a big place if God calls you there: that's a path followed by many seminary graduates.[16] But it is wrong to move to a small place *in order to prepare* to move to something better.

FREEDOM AND JOY WHEREVER WE SERVE

We can feel enormous freedom as we evaluate these reasons for small-place and big-place ministry. God may call us somewhere big for our whole lives, or he may call us to a joyful lifetime of small. Perhaps he wants us in a big place for a period of time followed by ministry in a small one or the other way around. We ought to stay open to his leading at every stage of our lives. He's called me to more than a decade of happy small-town ministry, and I have no plans to leave. But I hope I'll be ready if he ever sends me to a city or suburb.

Tim Keller strikes just the right balance when he writes about whether people ought to live and minister in the city (I'd be perfectly happy to substitute "a small place" for "the city" in what follows):

> God does not call everyone to live in a city, nor do those he calls to the city necessarily have to live their entire life there. People who find great opportunity to use their gifts productively elsewhere need to be able to go out from the city without guilt. People who for selfish or cowardly reasons will not even think of living in the city, however, need to be confronted. Consider it done.[17]

In addition to freedom, we can also feel enormous joy in our calling. Wherever God calls us to serve, our identity and significance are secure because we're his children. Our worth comes not from the place where we proclaim the gospel but from the gospel we proclaim. This gospel is equally precious, and we are equally treasured by God, in places mighty or miniscule.

Moreover, big-place and small-place pastors are on the same team—and this knowledge allows pastors and laypeople in small places to rejoice in what God is doing in the cities. In recent years I've visited friends deeply invested in city ministry and read many excellent blogs, articles, and books about city ministry. Again and again I've been inspired and overjoyed at what God is doing in the great cities of the world. In Psalm 48 we see God honoring and blessing his spectacular city, Mount Zion, the wonder of the whole world—and the villages and towns of Judah aren't jealous. Instead, they're jubilant, rejoicing along with the city. In the end, neither the city nor the country is ultimate: instead, it's God who gets the glory.

This is God,
our God forever and ever.
He will guide us forever. (Psalm 48:14)

12

Common Reasons to Prioritize Big-Place Ministry

S O FAR WE'VE CONSIDERED REASONS we *shouldn't* go to small places as well as reasons we *should* go and reasons we *don't* go. In this chapter, I'll take a slightly different approach. Rather than arguing we should or shouldn't go, I'll ask an overarching question, Is this really so? Let me explain.

PRIORITIZING THE CITY

In the past several decades a growing stream of what we might appreciatively call "urban apologetic literature" has emerged in Christian circles alongside a dynamic movement toward city ministry. The effect of this movement has been truly wonderful. The hearts of a generation of young church planters and church revitalizers have been fired for reaching the city. City churches have been planted, city souls have been won, cultures have been influenced, and the gospel has spread.[1] Though much gospel work remains to be done in the great cities, the gains are indisputable.

The blogs, articles, and books that form the urban apologetic literature usually affirm the importance of ministry everywhere, in places big and small.[2] But they also usually call for prioritizing city ministry. For example, Tim Keller writes, "We believe ministry in the center of global cities is the highest priority for the church in the twenty-first century."[3] What *priority* means is not usually explicitly stated. It may mean that (1) we ought to consider city ministry more important than we have in the past, or that (2) we ought to invest more resources and people in city ministry than we are at present.[4] But the word *priority* normally connotes something more than either of these. Perhaps it means that (3) we ought to consider city ministry more necessary and urgent than suburban or rural ministry, or even that (4) we ought to divert resources (money, people, ministries) away from the suburbs and small towns to the cities.

In some corners of evangelicalism, prioritizing cities has meant all four of these things and more. In practice (if not in theory) it has meant moving ministry headquarters and conferences from small places to big places and making key urban centers the major focus of denominational church planting efforts. In practice (if not in theory) it has meant sending the best and brightest Bible college and seminary graduates to the cities. In practice (if not in theory) it has meant that many Bible college and seminary students have come to *believe* that the best and brightest should go to the cities. Therefore, in practice (though certainly not in theory), it has meant city ministers sometimes look down on their country colleagues, and rural ministers sometimes envy their city colleagues, tacitly believing that their own ministries are second best. And in practice (though again, certainly not in theory) the playing field has been tilted to such a degree that many aspiring ministers never even consider the possibility that God may call them to minister long-term in a small place.

PROBING THE PRIORITY OF THE CITY

Too often urban and rural ministry have been pitted against one another, as though one must lose in order for the other to gain. I hope it's clear that I don't subscribe to that view. As I've said, I rejoice when I read books about city ministry and speak with friends who lead urban and suburban churches. I gladly invest both prayer and money in city ministry. Much of the urban apologetic literature is written by my ministry heroes and personal friends. In the spirit of friendship, then, and in hopes of fostering fruitful discussion, I'd like to consider some of the claims made in these writings and ask if this is really so. Urban apologetic literature provides many reasons for prioritizing the city. Most of them fall into three main categories, which I'll call the historical reason, the strategic reason, and the eschatological reason.

The historical reason: The apostle Paul and the other early Christian missionaries focused exclusively on ministry in cities. Early Christianity was an urban religion. The historical reason is expressed by Tim Keller in *Why God Made Cities*:

> Look at the New Testament. Historical research shows that the early Christian missionaries in the Roman Empire did not go to the countryside. They did not go to small towns. Paul was the best example of this. They went into the cities and only the cities to preach the gospel.[5]

Quotations such as this lead me to wonder whether, at times, the urban apologetic literature minimizes (or altogether ignores) the ministry of Jesus and his first disciples. For example, one urban ministry book describes Paul's city-focused ministry as the "New Testament plan."[6] But shouldn't Jesus' example be considered when describing the New Testament plan? Don't Jesus' first disciples qualify as "early Christian missionaries in the Roman Empire"? And didn't Jesus and his disciples spend lots of time in villages and the countryside?

Jesus and the Twelve. The gospels present a picture of Jesus' ministry as remarkably pervasive within his geographical area. It's not just that people came to Jesus from all over (Matthew 14:13; Luke 8:4; Mark 6:33), but Jesus himself went to them. He regularly ministered in cities and towns, villages and hamlets, the countryside and farms (Mark 6:56; Luke 8:1; 13:22).[7] In fact, we're told that Jesus visited *all* the towns and villages of Galilee (Matthew 9:35). He could easily have visited the 175 towns and villages of lower and upper Galilee during his ministry travels, and it's likely that a major portion of the two hundred thousand people living in Galilee personally saw him during his public ministry.[8] While these communities were connected with highly developed trade routes and were influenced to some degree by urbanization, almost all were nonetheless tiny and unimpressive.[9] For instance, Capernaum was a small village with between six hundred and fifteen hundred residents, while Nazareth had less than four hundred.[10] Jesus embraced his identity as "Jesus of Nazareth" (Luke 18:37; Acts 22:8) rather than avoiding association with a small place.[11]

It wasn't just Jesus who went to small places. When he sent out his twelve disciples, he anticipated that they would go to the towns and villages of Israel (Matthew 10:11), which is in fact where they went (Luke 9:6). There's no reason to believe that later Christian missionaries understood the small-place ministry of Jesus and his disciples as being eclipsed by the apostle Paul's urban-focused ministry. On the contrary, New Testament scholar Eckhard Schnabel suggests that the "early Christians certainly would have regarded . . . Jesus' ministry as the model for their own ministry" and that as early missionaries considered Jesus' commission, "they must have decided that their assignment included reaching as many people as possible in all the towns and villages in the regions that they would visit."[12] After all, Jesus' commands for gospel work in villages were preserved in the biblical Gospels, which were circulated *after* Paul's mission and death. As early Christians read these accounts, they were reminded of Jesus' care for small places and his commands to go there.[13]

What we don't know. Let's set to one side the example of Jesus and his first disciples. It's worth probing Keller's claim that Paul and the early Christian missionaries did not go to the countryside or small towns but only the cities. Is this really so? I wonder whether we should allow for less certainty, admitting what we don't actually know. For instance, there's scant information in the New Testament concerning the early period of Paul's missionary work.[14] Did he focus exclusively on cities during that period, or might he have done some mission work in small towns (as perhaps indicated by Acts 26:20)? For much of that period we simply don't know.

It's certainly true that in Luke's Acts account of Paul's ministry he focuses on Paul's engagement with leading cities. But can we be certain that's because Paul targeted only strategic urban centers? Might Luke's literary focus be shaped, at least in part, by other factors? After all, Luke quite clearly wanted to show his readers that Paul received good treatment from Roman officials, and that would have been a good reason for Luke to highlight Paul's experience in cities, where he encountered those officials.[15] It's clear that Luke sometimes reported information selectively.[16] In fact, from Paul's letters we know of "churches of Judea that are in Christ" (Galatians 1:22; cf. 1 Thessalonians 2:14), a phrase that likely refers to many small congregations in the villages and towns of Judea, even though Luke focuses on Jerusalem in the book of Acts, not mentioning these churches.[17] Responding to the view that Paul engaged in "urban mission, not in village or rural mission," Schnabel concludes, "This view may be historically correct, but it remains hypothetical because neither Paul nor Luke provides a complete picture of Paul's missionary methods."[18]

What we do know. In fact, it seems nearly certain that Paul *did* preach in villages during his missionary travels.[19] We're told that after Paul and Barnabas were expelled from Iconium, they preached to the cities of Lystra and Derbe as well as the towns and villages they controlled (Acts 14:6-7). Paul himself, in his address to King Agrippa, claimed that after his conversion he preached "to those in Damascus, then in Jerusalem and throughout all the region of Judea, and also to the Gentiles" (Acts 26:20).[20] Indeed, Paul must have traveled frequently and extensively through the countryside. The cities of his day were "dots on a rural landscape," and of course he couldn't hop between them on a plane.[21] (In some cases he could travel by boat, but Acts 20:13 shows an instance of him opting for land travel instead.) When he passed through the villages and countryside, Paul surely must have shared the good news with those he met.[22] He would have passed thousands of rural temples, major attractions in the countryside, which it's difficult to imagine him not engaging.[23] For these reasons it's inadequate to describe Paul's work as a "metropolis mission."[24]

Did Paul go to cities because they were strategic? Let's assume for the sake of argument that Paul did in fact focus exclusively on urban centers. Can we be sure *why*? One influential view is that Paul aimed to establish strategic centers of influence in cities, from which the surrounding countryside could then be reached. Most famously advocated by Roland Allen in his 1912 book *Missionary Methods: St. Paul's or Ours?* this view has often been repeated since.[25] It's frequently endorsed in the urban apologetic literature, which claims that Paul and the early missionaries avoided the countryside because of its conservative nature and preached the gospel exclusively in cities because their strategic influence facilitated the dissemination of ideas, the spread of converts, and broader cultural transformation—all of which led to the eventual winning of the countryside.[26] In fact, it's often claimed that the reason the early church "captured the Roman Empire" and won the world was because it went to the cities.[27]

The city-as-strategic-center view of Paul's ministry has some evidence to commend it. Both Acts and Paul's letters indicate that Paul spent time in commercial, cultural, and religious centers. Moreover, several New Testament passages (e.g., Acts 19:8-10; Romans 15:18-20) are often interpreted to imply that Paul viewed his task as establishing urban centers of Christian influence in order to reach the countryside. Nevertheless, it's worth asking some questions.

First, assuming that Paul targeted cities, can we be sure that he did so because of their strategic value? Might other factors have been at play? For instance, might Paul have gone to cities because of his commitment to speak the gospel to Jews, since that's where the Jewish populations outside of Judea lived?[28] Might he have gone to cities rather than the countryside in regions where he couldn't speak the provincial dialect since Greek was more likely to be spoken in the city?[29] If Paul was committed to cities for their strategic value, why did he sometimes bypass important cities in his travels?[30] Schnabel suggests that, while there was strategic value in planting churches in cities, it is "a significant over-statement to say that Paul's passion was the planting of churches in metropolitan centers or in the 'strategic cities' of the Roman Empire."[31] Many of the cities where Paul preached were organized as *poleis*, or Greek city-states, and would have had limited influence beyond their own territories. Moreover, each city fostered its own identity; cities competed with one another and would therefore have resisted influence from other cities.[32]

Second, was it really the case that Paul avoided the countryside because it was too conservative? Thomas Robinson has raised serious questions about this view.[33] In fact, the presence of early Christians in the countryside shows that it was *not* impossible for Christianity to break through rural barriers. We know of examples of contemporary prophets, healers, and exorcists who were successful in the countryside, and this suggests it was not as conservative as is supposed.[34] In fact, it could be argued that the cities, which were centers of religious influence and power, would have had more to lose from a new religion and would therefore have been more inherently conservative than the countryside.[35]

Is there evidence of early Christians in rural areas? What about other early Christian missionaries besides Paul? Keller mentions historical research showing they did not go to the countryside or small towns but only the cities. He's referring to what has been called the urban thesis of Christian origins, a view that has been influential in New Testament scholarship as well as evangelical writing about city ministry.[36] According to many proponents of the urban thesis, early Christianity was an almost exclusively urban reality, spreading to the countryside in the fourth century only after Emperor Constantine's influence was sufficient to convert the conservative countryside. Rodney Stark asserts that it was several centuries until the church conducted a significant missionary enterprise in the countryside and says, "Any study of how Christians converted the empire is really a study of how they Christianized the cities."[37]

But Thomas Robinson has recently offered a major and convincing critique of the urban thesis, showing an early Christian presence in the countryside before the year AD 250. I've already noted the rural nature of the ministries of Jesus and his earliest disciples, but Robinson's case extends far beyond that. There's evidence of early rural Christianity in Asia Minor, Egypt, North Africa, and Syria,[38] and a number of first- and second-century writers noted the rural presence of early Christians and early Christian mission.[39] For example, in the mid-90s AD, Clement of Rome mentioned the early apostles preaching "throughout the countryside and in the cities."[40] In the early second century, the

Roman governor Pliny said that Christianity had spread not just to cities but to "villages and country districts."[41] Justin Martyr, in the middle of the second century, claimed that "there is not a single race of human beings, barbarians, Greeks, or whatever name you please to call them, nomads or vagrants or herdsmen living in tents where prayers in the name of Jesus are not offered up."[42] In another writing, he spoke of Christians meeting on Sundays in cities and villages.[43] All this evidence shows there's good reason to believe that Christianity—and some form of Christian mission—was present early in the countryside even when Luke doesn't mention it in Acts and when we don't find a record of it in some early sources.[44]

Questions of application. To this point I've raised historical questions regarding the claim that Paul and the early missionaries went only to cities. But even assuming we grant that claim, big questions remain regarding how to *apply* it. In urban apologetic literature, Paul's practice is usually assumed to be an example for us to follow. But is it meant that way? This raises the distinction between what is descriptive and prescriptive in the Bible (particularly in narrative books such as Acts).[45] Unlike the clear commands from Jesus to his disciples to go into towns and villages, Paul never commanded anyone to focus on cities, nor did he explain why he himself was drawn to cities. We can guess, but shouldn't the fact that we're guessing make us more hesitant to consider Paul's city ministry as normative for us?

Let's grant that the example of Paul and the early Christian missionaries is indeed meant to be followed by contemporary Christians. Then we need to ask *which* example? On the city-as-strategic-center view of Paul's ministry, Paul sent his coworkers out into the rural regions that surrounded the cities where he ministered. Drawing on Paul's ministry in Ephesus, which led to "all the residents of Asia" hearing the word of the Lord (Acts 19:10), Jon Dennis describes Paul's ministry as "winning, training and sending."[46] Leaving aside the real possibility that Paul himself traveled from Ephesus into the countryside, and assuming that Dennis's description is correct, why do so many contemporary church planters take Paul, rather than his associates, as their model? Couldn't passages such as Acts 19:10 and Romans 15:19, often taken as a call to follow Paul to the city, equally be heard as a call to follow the unknown associates of Paul *out* of the city and into the countryside?

The strategic reason: It's strategic to establish city churches because cities shape culture. Gospel influence will radiate from the city into the countryside but not vice versa. The strategic reason is, of course, closely related to the historical one. It's often claimed that Paul and the early Christians established city churches because of their strategic value for reaching the countryside *and that we should do the same.*[47] I've already asked several questions about the historicity and normative status of Paul's focus on strategic cities. Now it's worth asking whether going to the cities is actually an effective way of reaching the small places today.

Alan Barth articulates the strategic reason as it's commonly expressed in the urban apologetic literature: "Whatever develops in the city tends to have a profound effect throughout the nation and often the world. Influence tends to move from the city outward, not inward."[48] It's often thought that the spread of influence (and gospel influence in particular) occurs in two main ways. First, through the movement of *people* who come to the city and then return to the countryside.[49] Second, through the shaping of the broader culture, which occurs both through "identifying deeply with the poor" and by reaching urban cultural elites and institutions.[50]

But is reaching the city actually an effective strategy for reaching the countryside? We've already seen that in order to reach small places, Jesus and his early followers chose to *go* to small places. For several reasons, I'm not so sure that the city's shaping of culture and flow of people will get the gospel to small places.

Let's consider first the city's cultural influence. It's true that cultural influence generally moves from city to country rather than in the opposite direction. My small town certainly tends to follow fashion trends (albeit somewhat tardily) rather than form them. But it's equally clear that rural culture isn't *always* influenced by cities. The surprising 2016 election of Donald Trump demonstrated that. In fact, the Brookings Institution spoke at the time of a "growing divide" between those who live in and those who live outside large metropolitan areas.[51] This divide wasn't *created* by Trump; on the contrary, it's one of the factors that got him elected. Already in 2012 one commentator observed, "The new political divide is a stark division between cities and what remains of the countryside."[52]

An even more basic question concerns the effectiveness of broad, indirect cultural influence in promoting widespread *gospel* influence. Even assuming Christians can influence urban elites and institutions, will that promote the movement of the gospel to small places? Doesn't the spread of the gospel usually occur through personal influence? Importantly, the urban apologetic literature clearly and frequently recognizes the unique power of personal, face-to-face interaction for business, technology, the arts, and many other forms of human flourishing.[53] We might have thought that newly available technologies would incline young people to work remotely from homes in the quiet countryside, but the importance of immediate, personal influence explains why they keep coming to cities. A 2015 *Newsweek* article titled "Why Millennials Still Move to Cities" noted that "Breakthrough ideas come from connections between people and their ideas, and more connections create exponentially more ideas." Richard Florida calls this the "clustering force," and Edward Glaeser suggests that the success of cities "depends on the demand for physical connection." Knowledge is "best produced by people in close proximity to other people."[54]

If this is true, shouldn't it incline us to look not just for broad, indirect cultural influence but to where *people* are flowing? The flow is mainly in one direction: as the McKinsey Global Institute noted in a 2011 report, "The world is in the throes of a sweeping population shift from the countryside to the city."[55] This overall movement from small places to big places suggests the neglected possibility of lots of *personal* influence moving from small places to big places. If that's the case, is reaching the small places best done by going to the cities? Isn't it urgently important to go to the small places themselves, live face-to-face with the people there, and seek to influence them with the gospel? Maybe reaching small places is best done not by going to cities but to small places.

There's a gospel opportunity here for small-place ministers. Many of the young people in small-place churches will move away to college and never return. They'll settle in the urban centers of the world. But for the first, formative period of their lives, small-place churches will have the sacred opportunity to shape them profoundly. Robert Wuthnow writes of the "portable values" that small-town residents internalize and take with them into the big cities when they move away.[56] What if those values aren't just honesty, thrift, and hard work, but an abiding passion for the gospel of Jesus Christ? Forgotten places can shape and send gospel-loving young people on mission to the cities of the world. We can influence big places from small ones.

While many young people migrate away from the city centers as they grow older, most settle in the suburbs rather than continuing outward to the small towns and countryside.[57] The personal, gospel influence they will exercise in the suburbs is noted in the urban apologetic literature as a reason for the centrality and priority of urban ministry.[58] But might this same logic not also demonstrate (given the massive flow of young people to cities) the importance and influence of faithful small-place ministry?

Of course, general population flows may not reflect the current work of city churches who aim to reach small places with the gospel. But the stories of "radiating influence" I've heard tend to be from the city to the suburbs, not to the small towns. City churches are planting into suburbs, but are they planting (are they even *aiming* to plant) rural, small-town churches? Strikingly, in the course of a discussion about how Paul sent people to the whole province of Asia, one urban pastor shares how his church has sent people to other cities. In fact, the stated aim of church-planting organizations like Redeemer City to City is not from the city to small towns but from one city to another.[59] This differs from the vision of Roland Allen, who called for city churches to be "centers of light" for the surrounding countryside.[60] I wonder if there's a bit of tension for the city-as-strategic-center advocates here. One stated reason for prioritizing city ministry is that it can move the gospel from the city to the countryside. But getting the gospel from the city to the small towns requires sending people from the city to the countryside, which is generally the *opposite* of what the urban apologetic literature calls for, with its exhortations to prioritize the cities and move into them. (It's often noted that the movement of Christians to the cities is not keeping up with the growth of cities.)

Here's a final question regarding strategy: assuming city-center churches develop a clear vision and passion for planting rural and small-town churches, are they equipped for this work? We've seen that in both our broader culture and urban church culture there are significant misunderstandings about small towns and rural communities. It can be particularly difficult for people from the city to fit into a small town.[61] That's because city culture is different from even nearby country areas and towns.[62] "Living in Atlanta resembles living in Boston more than it does life in rural

Georgia. Small-town Porterville, California, has more in common with upstate New York towns than with Los Angeles, just two hours away."[63] This reality, which is recognized in the urban apologetic literature, complicates the task of a city church longing to be a center of light for the surrounding countryside.[64]

The eschatological reason: The end-time destiny of the people of God is life in a city. The frequent claim among urban ministry advocates that God's people are destined for life in a city is based on John's vision and description of the new Jerusalem in Revelation 21–22. Drawing on this passage, the urban apologetic literature includes several variations on the claim that our future will be an *urban* future. Some writers simply state that all God's people will live in a city, without qualifying or nuancing that claim.[65] It's also sometimes said that humankind began in a garden but will end in a city.[66] Other writers describe a mainly urban future for God's people while allowing the possibility that the future may not be *exclusively* urban.[67] Still others recognize that the new Jerusalem isn't only urban but rather a kind of "garden city," the Garden of Eden finally cultivated and brought to fulfillment.[68]

Variations on this theme are used to support a couple of related claims. First, despite the frequently negative biblical descriptions of cities, from Babel in Genesis to Babylon in Revelation, God neither despises cities per se nor plans to do away with cities in the new creation. Second, our final urban future calls for the prioritization of city ministry in the present. The first point seems indisputable. It's the second one I'd like to probe. Does the description of the new Jerusalem in Revelation 21–22 actually support the prioritization of urban ministry?

Let's assume that John sees an exclusively urban new Jerusalem—he does, after all, refer to it repeatedly as a city. Does John specify that everyone in the new creation will be urban residents? Might the city he sees be set in the surrounding countryside,

as ancient Levitical cities were (Leviticus 25:34), indeed, as Ezekiel's end-time vision of God's future city was (Ezekiel 48:15-20)?
John doesn't tell us one way or the other. Nor does he say that all
the inhabitants of the new heaven and earth live in the city. The
kings of the earth and those who are written in the Lamb's book of
life enter the city (Revelation 21:24, 27), but that doesn't mean
they stay there. The gates are open; perhaps there's regular
movement in and out (Revelation 21:25). God clearly dwells in the
city, but surely his people can enjoy his glory wherever they are
throughout the new creation.

It's even more important to ask what exactly the new Jerusalem *is*. Two of its most striking features are the "river of the
water of life, bright as crystal" that flows through the middle of
the street, and the tree of life with its twelve kinds of fruit,
yielding its fruit in each month (Revelation 22:1-2, 19). These features show that the new Jerusalem is clearly Eden revisited. The
Old Testament prophets sometimes pictured God's final future as
a garden, using themes of agricultural abundance. Some have suggested that John draws on that prophetic picture and that in
Revelation the city of God and Garden of Eden have coalesced.[69]

Brad Roth makes an even more intriguing suggestion. In the
prophet Ezekiel's vision of the future Zion, water flows from the
temple out of the city; it's out there in the green space surrounding
the city (Ezekiel 48:15-20) that Ezekiel sees trees with leaves that
don't wither, with fresh fruit in every month (Ezekiel 47:12).
John, like Ezekiel, sees the river inside the city. But unlike Ezekiel,
John also sees the ever-fruitful tree of life *inside* the city
(Revelation 22:2). In Roth's words, "The garden is downtown.
Zion no longer stands centered on [the surrounding green space].
In John's retrofitted vision, the [surrounding green space] has
come inside. . . . The holy rural has been brought into the heart of
the holy city."[70] In other words, John's vision is of a garden-city,
and the garden part isn't less important than the city part. John

sees our future as a rural-urban future in which countryside and city mingle, for the good of both and the blessing of all.

If this is so, we may ask about the implications of John's vision for our present ministry. As Brad Roth notes, contemporary discussions within the church sometimes encounter rural-urban fault lines. For example, discussions of faithful sexual practice may run up against urban progressivism and rural conservatism. To the extent that urban churches see themselves as the "vanguard of the church," they will privilege their own views and instincts.[71] But if John's vision is of a garden-city, rural and urban interwoven and coalesced, mutually benefiting one another, we're pointed toward a future in which rural and urban need one another forever. Neither is complete without the other. That's true not just in the final future but in the present.

PUSHING BACK ON PRIORITIZING

I don't pretend to have answered (or even asked) all the important questions regarding whether city ministry ought to be prioritized. I've simply made a start at what I hope will be a charitable, gracious conversation regarding an important topic—a significant topic for building a theological vision for ministry in small places. But I have enough questions regarding the case for prioritizing city ministry that I think it's worth pushing back on this view as it's commonly expressed. I'd prefer to speak about the crucial importance of big-place ministry and the crucial importance of small-place ministry (and all the places in between), without prioritizing either one. It's best to leave it to God to prioritize the city, suburbs, or countryside in each individual life. If God calls you to the city, throw yourself fully into ministry there. If he calls you to a suburb, don't flee to a city or small town. If he calls you to the countryside, make it your priority to gladly serve him there.

Conclusion

PRAY BIG, TRUST GOD, WORK HARD

SEVERAL YEARS AGO I visited dear friends who have labored among Muslims for many years. They live with their four children in an ancient, sprawling city in the Middle East where the falafel makers are busy and the mosques sound their calls to prayer loudly and often. My friends moved to their current home because the country in which they previously lived had become unsafe, and they knew refugees would soon pour over the border. They were right: the refugees have come, and my friends visit them daily, building friendships, sharing Bible stories, and meeting any needs they can. Their ministry has required enormous effort and sacrifice. They've learned Arabic, moved numerous times, and are raising their children far from extended family, friends, and the conveniences of home. Churches and individuals back home have provided hundreds of thousands of dollars over many years to support their work. It's stunning to consider the investment of energy, funding, prayer, and personal sacrifice required to get them where they are and keep them there.

And for what? Their work is small, slow, and seemingly unstrategic. They've seen few conversions. During my visit, we spent many hours with a Muslim man very dear to my friend, and it became clear that this man was still far from the gospel. Later, my friend expressed his discouragement to me. Viewed in terms of results, the ministry of this remarkable family seems like a waste.

But what if we evaluate their ministry in terms of its gospel shape and its see-throughability to the glory of God and the beauty of his gospel? Things begin to look different. My friends' ministry is expressing something of God and his gospel that couldn't be expressed through a massive revival. All their many sacrifices, their unconditional friendship offered to a young Muslim family still blind to the glory of Christ, their consistent, prayerful sharing of the gospel with those who will listen—these things are living demonstrations of a generous God and a lavish gospel. The gospel announces the infinite sacrifice God will make to reach just one person, and this divine love is being imaged through my friends. They're like the shepherd searching for his lost sheep in a gully and the woman groping under the couch for her coin. Their lives are reflecting God's patient pursuit, his kindness to those who reject him, his work that advances even when it seems stalled. Their ministry is necessary for the church of Jesus Christ because the church without a witness in Muslim countries (and in many other difficult, marginal contexts) is not the church as God intends it to be. We need the small, the slow, the church on the margins, in order to present a full picture of God and his gospel.

To be sure, my friends don't idolize what is small and slow. Surprisingly, it's entirely possible to do just that. Some of us have noticed an odd thing happening at gatherings of rural pastors and laypeople. We've seen pastors bragging not about how *large* their churches are (as often happens at conferences) but about the *smallness* of their towns, one-upping each other in a kind of race to the bottom ("*My* town is so small that the last one to bed at night turns out the street light!"). At one such gathering, I had my small-town cred called into question by a couple who insisted that Pepperell really doesn't qualify as a small town. (The subtext was that if I really wanted to see a small town, I should check out where *they're* ministering.)

The tendency to brag about the smallness of our place, making it a badge of honor to display, is an important reminder that human beings can turn anything into an idol, a false means of distinction and self-exaltation. My friends in the Middle East aren't doing that. They long for *many* people to know Jesus, and they'd love it to happen *fast*. They pray regularly for a great movement of people to Christ. If God does that, he will demonstrate his infinite power, his great mercy, and his sovereign call.

Both visible success and the lack of it are opportunities for my friends to display God's worth. In this season of their ministry, God has given them the latter. What if God has done the same for you in your small place? I don't assume that he has. You may be experiencing clearly visible success: conversions, maturing Christians, transformed communities, new church plants. Your ministry may be like William Grimshaw of Haworth.

But what if it's more like Tom Carson of Quebec or George Herbert of Bemerton? What if it's small, slow, and seemingly unstrategic? Do you need something more, or can you be content? Will you pray boldly with faith for God to win many souls for his glory and simultaneously see your present situation as a glorious display of the character of God and the surpassing beauty of the gospel? Rather than gazing longingly at the big places where so much ministry seems to be happening, will you see all the ministry to be done right in front of you? Will you treasure the people in your small place and pour yourself out for them? Will you prepare eternal souls for eternity?

Marilynne Robinson's fictional pastor John Ames stays in little Gilead, Iowa, his entire life, despite the urging of others to "wake from the trance" and gain "broader experience" by leaving. As an old man, he writes a long letter to the child he knows is too young to remember him after he dies. Reflecting on his long life and ministry in Gilead, Ames writes,

> To me it seems rather Christlike to be as unadorned as this place is, as little regarded. . . . I love this town. I think sometimes of going into the ground here as a last wild gesture of

love—I too will smolder away the time until the great and general incandescence.[1]

"I love this town." At the heart of every successful ministry, in communities of every conceivable size, is love: love for Christ and for the places where he has called us. When we truly love a particular place and the people who live there, we won't seek to transcend it—instead, we will gladly give our lives to it. Perhaps we can learn to love our small places the way Jesus does. Perhaps in losing our lives there, we will find them.

Acknowledgments

I'M THANKFUL TO MANY FRIENDS AND MINISTRY PARTNERS for shaping this book. Thanks, Matt Chambers, for all your help with Small Town Summits. The Gospel Guys have been a great encouragement to me (thanks to Paul Buckley for coming up with some of my chapter titles on a Panera napkin!), as have Donnie Griggs and the men of the Small Town Jesus cohort (special thanks to Ty DesEnfants, Ben Franks, and Scott Berg for their help). Paul Jump, Paul Mathole, and Jonathan Dodson, three dear friends who also happen to be city pastors, read drafts and made helpful suggestions. Ministry partnerships and long conversations with Jeff Willett, John Standridge, Tyler Yates, Mike Rattin, Josh Rattin, Dustin Shramek, and Keith and Bonnie Greer have shaped my pastoring and thinking. My brothers, Tim and Andrew Witmer, were my constant companions while growing up in a small town. Andrew has been an amazingly good conversation partner in this project, sharing new thoughts and pointing me to resources I hadn't seen. I've dedicated the book to my parents, Daryl and Mary Witmer, who first introduced me to the gospel and also modeled integrity and godliness in small-town ministry over the course of decades. Ethan McCarthy and the team at InterVarsity Press have been a delight to work with and have made the book much better than it was when I gave it to them.

I presented portions of this book at the Center for Pastor Theologians, the Evangelical Theological Society Ecclesiology group, the Bangor Pastor Theologians gathering, the Rural Home Missionary Association, the Gospel Coalition national conference, and the Small Town Jesus conference, and I'm grateful for the feedback and interaction of those who heard my talks. I'm also thankful to the Gospel Coalition and Desiring God for publishing several of my articles on small-town ministry, some of which have been adapted and used in this book.[1]

I love serving the people of Pepperell Christian Fellowship and have been formed deeply by a decade of ministry in our small town. PCF is consistently and remarkably kind and gracious to me and my family, and I'm thankful to God for calling us to our church family. Thanks to the elders and congregation for granting us a sabbatical in the United Kingdom in summer 2018 so that I could write this book. Thanks also to my parents-in-law, Leslie and Heather Hutchinson, for their help and hospitality during our sabbatical. And thanks to the generous friends and family who gave me the use of their cottages and homes to write: Hazel and Mervyn McCall, Hugh and Ann McCormick, Jonathan and Susan McFerrin, and Jim and Jen Simpson. Also, thanks, Caffè Nero at Ballyhackamore, for letting me use the big table.

Much of this book has grown from the work I do with my dear friends David Pinckney and Ben Ruhl as we lead Small Town Summits together. Thanks for your friendship, David and Ben. It's a great joy to partner with you, and what a thrill it's been for us to meet so many choice servants of God who are serving in small places throughout New England.

My wife, Emma, grew up in a city in Northern Ireland and moved with me to a small town in Massachusetts. Thank you, Emma, for being my best friend and partner in everything I do. I love you deeply. To our kids, Samuel, Annie, and Henry, you give me immense joy and enrich my life immeasurably. I pray that you'll embrace the great big gospel of Jesus Christ your whole lives long.

INTRODUCTION

[1]See Harvie M. Conn and Manuel Ortiz, *Urban Ministry* (Downers Grove, IL: IVP Academic, 2001), 233-51.

[2]Conn and Ortiz, *Urban Ministry*, 235.

[3]Tish Harrison Warren, "I Overlooked the Rural Poor—Then Trump Came Along," *Christianity Today*, August 22, 2016, www.christianitytoday.com /ct/2016/september/i-overlooked-rural-poor-then-trump-came-along .html.

[4]Amanda Abrams, "The Pastors Out to Save Millennials' Souls," *Daily Beast*, July 10, 2016, www.thedailybeast.com/the-pastors-out-to-save-millennials -souls.

1. TAKING A FRESH LOOK AT SMALL PLACES

[1]Chad Shearer, "The Small Town-Big City Split That Elected Donald Trump," *Brookings*, November 11, 2016, www.brookings.edu/blog/the-avenue/2016 /11/11/the-small-town-big-city-split-that-elected-donald-trump.

[2]Andy Beckett, "From Trump to Brexit, Power Has Leaked from Cities to the Countryside," *Guardian*, December 12, 2016, www.theguardian.com /commentisfree/2016/dec/12/trump-brexit-cities-countryside-rural-voters.

[3]Rick Noac, "The Urban-Rural Divide That Bolstered Trump Isn't Just an American Thing; It's Prevalent in Europe, Too," *Washington Post*, November 27, 2016, www.washingtonpost.com/news/worldviews/wp/2016/11 /27/the-urban-rural-divide-isnt-just-evident-in-american-politics-its -prevalent-in-europe-too.

[4]"World Urbanization Prospects: The 2014 Revision," United Nations, 2014, 1, https://esa.un.org/unpd/wup/publications/files/wup2014-highlights .pdf.

[5]Alan Smith and Jill Hopkinson, eds., *Faith and the Future of the Countryside* (Norwich, UK: Canterbury Press, 2012), xiv.

[6]"The Spiritual Landscape of New England," Vision New England and Gordon-Conwell Theological Seminary, September 15, 2017, https:// slideplayer.com/slide/15189832.

[7]Mark Easton, "How Much of Your Area Is Built On?" *BBC News*, November 9, 2017, www.bbc.co.uk/news/uk-41901294; and Kenneth Johnson, "Rural

America Undergoing a Diversity of Demographic Change," *Population Reference Bureau*, May 1, 2006, www.prb.org/ruralamericaundergoingadi versityofdemographicchange.

[8]Stephen T. Um and Justin Buzzard, *Why Cities Matter* (Wheaton, IL: Crossway, 2013), 9.

[9]Brad Roth, *God's Country: Faith, Hope and the Future of the Rural Church* (Harrisonburg, VA: Herald Press, 2017), 26.

[10]"World Urbanization Prospects," 4.

[11]In his book *Small-Town America*, sociologist Robert Wuthnow focuses on small towns of less than twenty-five thousand people not part of an urbanized area. By that definition, there are 33.7 million Americans living in small towns. Adding small towns in urban fringe areas results in an additional four thousand towns containing 23 million more people. See Robert Wuthnow, *Small-Town America* (Princeton, NJ: Princeton University Press, 2015).

[12]Pamela Riney-Kehrberg, ed., *The Routledge History of Rural America* (New York: Routledge, 2016), 2.

[13]Roth, *God's Country*, 27.

[14]"Massachusetts Community Types," Metropolitan Area Planning Council, July 2008, www.mapc.org/wp-content/uploads/2017/09/Massachusetts -Community-Types-Summary-July_2008.pdf.

[15]Timothy Keller, *Making Sense of God* (New York: Penguin, 2018), 24.

[16]Donnie Griggs, *Small Town Jesus* (Damascus, MD: EverTruth, 2016), 57-58.

2. WHY SMALL PLACES ARE BETTER THAN WE THINK

[1]Bill Bryson, *The Lost Continent: Travels in Small-Town America* (London: Transworld, 2015), 59.

[2]Janet Adamy and Paul Overberg, "Rural America Is the New 'Inner City,'" *Wall Street Journal*, May 26, 2017, www.wsj.com/articles/rural-america-is -the-new-inner-city-1495817008.

[3]"World Urbanization Prospects: The 2014 Revision," United Nations, 2014, https://esa.un.org/unpd/wup/publications/files/wup2014-highlights .pdf, 7.

[4]David B. Danbom, *Born in the Country*, 2nd ed. (Baltimore: Johns Hopkins University Press, 2006), 250.

[5]Victor Davis Hanson, "The Oldest Divide," *City Journal*, autumn 2015, www.city-journal.org/html/oldest-divide-14042.html. According to professor David Danbom, more than half of rural Americans were farmers at

the end of World War II; by the early twenty-first century only 7 percent were (Danbom, *Born in the Country*, 247).

[6]Richard Hofstadter, quoted in Minoa Uffelman, "Teaching Rural History in an Urban Age," in *The Routledge History of Rural America*, ed. Pamela Riney-Kehrberg (New York: Routledge, 2016), 368.

[7]Emily Badger, "As American as Apple Pie? The Rural Vote's Disproportionate Slice of Power," *New York Times*, November 20, 2016, www.nytimes .com/2016/11/21/upshot/as-american-as-apple-pie-the-rural-votes -disproportionate-slice-of-power.html.

[8]Tom Vilsack, quoted in Christopher Doering, "As More Move to the City, Does Rural America Still Matter?" *USA Today*, January 13, 2013, https ://eu.usatoday.com/story/news/nation/2013/01/12/rural-decline -congress/1827407.

[9]Wendell Berry, *Jayber Crow* (Washington, DC: Counterpoint, 2000), 139.

[10]Jack Williams, *Easy On, Easy Off: The Urban Pathology of America's Small Towns* (Charlottesville: University of Virginia Press, 2016), 278.

[11]Cynthia M. Duncan, *Worlds Apart: Poverty and Politics in Rural America*, 2nd ed. (New Haven, CT: Yale University Press, 2014), xi.

[12]Robert Samuels, "A Week After Hurricane Michael, Rural Residents Feel-Stranded," *Washington Post*, October 18, 2018, www.washingtonpost.com /national/a-week-after-hurricane-michael-rural-residents-feel-stranded /2018/10/18/6cea4cb0-d2e4-11e8-8c22-fa2ef74bd6d6_story.html?no redirect=on&utm_term=.e73ddda5e10f.

[13]Sarah Pulliam Bailey, "Some Evangelicals Question Whether They Have Overlooked the Rural Church," *Washington Post*, December 15, 2016, www.washingtonpost.com/news/acts-of-faith/wp/2016/12/15/some -evangelicals-question-whether-they-have-overlooked-the-rural-church /?utm_term=.3c13780d0388.

[14]Amanda Abrams, "The Pastors Out to Save Millennials' Souls," *Daily Beast*, July 10, 2016, www.thedailybeast.com/the-pastors-out-to-save-millennials -souls.

[15]Tish Harrison Warren, "I Overlooked the Rural Poor—Then Trump Came Along," *Christianity Today*, August 22, 2016, www.christianitytoday.com /ct/2016/september/i-overlooked-rural-poor-then-trump-came-along .html.

[16]Ramsay MacMullen, cited in Thomas A. Robinson, *Who Were the First Christians? Dismantling the Urban Thesis* (New York: Oxford University Press, 2016), 123.

[17]Richard Bauckham, *Gospel of Glory* (Grand Rapids: Baker Academic, 2015), 163.

[18]Bauckham, *Gospel of Glory*, 163.

[19]Barack Obama, quoted in Jeff Zeleny, "Opponents Call Obama Remarks 'Out of Touch,'" *New York Times*, April 12, 2008, www.nytimes.com/2008 /04/12/us/politics/12campaign.html.

[20]Emmett Rensin, "The Smug Style in American Liberalism," *Vox*, April 21, 2016, www.vox.com/2016/4/21/11451378/smug-american-liberalism.

[21]Robert Wuthnow, *Small-Town America* (Princeton, NJ: Princeton University Press, 2015), 129.

[22]Robert Wuthnow, *The Left Behind: Decline and Rage in Rural America* (Princeton, NJ: Princeton University Press, 2018), 95-115.

[23]Robert Wuthnow, quoted in Sean Illing, "A Princeton Sociologist Spent 8 Years Asking Rural Americans Why They're So Pissed Off," *Vox*, June 30, 2018, www.vox.com/2018/3/13/17053886/trump-rural-america-populism -racial-resentment. See also Wuthnow, *Left Behind*, 11.

[24]Thomas Jefferson, quoted in Michael Swinford, "Urban-Rural Tensions, 1880-1930" in Riney-Kehrberg, *The Routledge History of Rural America*, 245.

[25]Swinford, "Urban-Rural Tensions," 245.

[26]Hanson, "The Oldest Divide."

[27]H. L. Mencken, quoted in Swinford, "Urban-Rural Tensions," 245.

[28]Michael J. Kruger, "The Arrogance of the Urban," *Cannon Fodder* (blog), June 5, 2012, www.michaeljkruger.com/the-arrogance-of-the-urban.

[29]Tim Keller, "The Country Parson," *Gospel Coalition*, December 2, 2009, www .thegospelcoalition.org/article/the-country-parson.

[30]David Van Biema, "Rural Churches Grapple with a Pastor Exodus," *Time*, January 29, 2009, http://content.time.com/time/magazine/article/0,9171 ,1874843,00.html.

[31]Jared Wilson, "Rural Ministry Is Not Second Rate," *Gospel Coalition*, June 5, 2012.

[32]John L. Thompson, *Urban Impact* (Eugene, OR: Wipf and Stock, 2011), 22.

[33]Francis Schaeffer, *No Little People* (Downers Grove, IL: InterVarsity Press, 1974), 14.

[34]Dante Chinni, "Rural Youth Chase Big-City Dreams," *Wall Street Journal*, June 26, 2017, www.wsj.com/articles/rural-youth-chase-big-city-dreams -1498478401.

[35]Patrick J. Carr and Maria J. Kefalas, *Hollowing Out the Middle: The Rural Brain Drain and What It Means for America* (Boston: Beacon Press, 2009), 109.

[36]Wendell Berry, "God and Country," in *What Are People For?* (Berkeley, CA: Counterpoint, 2010), 97.

[37]See David McGranahan, "Natural Amenities Drive Rural Population Change," Agricultural Economic Report No. 781, USDA; and Kenneth Johnson, "Rural America Undergoing a Diversity of Demographic Change," *Population Reference Bureau*, May 1, 2006, www.prb.org/ruralamericaunder goingadiversityofdemographicchange.

[38]Julianne Couch, *The Small-Town Midwest* (Iowa City: University of Iowa Press, 2016), 42.

[39]Maureen Milliken, "Libra Foundation's Monson Development on Track for First Artists," *Mainebiz*, April 25, 2018, www.mainebiz.biz/article/2018 0425/NEWS01/180429968/libra-foundation%27s-monson-development -on-track-for-first-artists.

[40]Dennis Gilbert, "Bio," *The Art of Alan Bray*, accessed April 10, 2019, www .alanbray.com/bio.

[41]Kathleen Norris, *Dakota* (New York: Houghton Mifflin Harcourt, 2001), 3.

[42]James Fallows and Deborah Fallows, *Our Towns* (New York: Pantheon, 2018), 397.

[43]Sarah Warwick and Anastasia Miari, "How to Save a Town," *N Magazine*, 67-74.

[44]Couch, *Small-Town Midwest*, 3, 48.

[45]David Brooks, "I Dream of Denver," *New York Times*, February 16, 2009, www.nytimes.com/2009/02/17/opinion/17brooks.html.

[46]Conor Macauley, "People in Northern Ireland's Rural Areas 'Are Happier,'" *BBC News*, September 27, 2017, www.bbc.co.uk/news/uk-northern -ireland-41397806; and University of Nebraska's survey of two thousand nonmetropolitan households, cited in Randy Cantrell, "The Rural Mindset," *National Association of Evangelicals*, fall 2017, 18-19, www.nae.net/the-rural -mindset.

[47]Christopher Ingraham, "People Who Live in Small Towns and Rural Areas Are Happier Than Everyone Else, Researchers Say," *Washington Post*, May 17, 2018, www.washingtonpost.com/news/wonk/wp/2018/05/17/people -who-live-in-small-towns-and-rural-areas-are-happier-than-everyone-else -researchers-say/?noredirect=on&utm_term=.bd1dbe759229. Not all social scientists are convinced of a correlation between rurality and happiness; some older studies concluded there wasn't one. See Donald M. Crider, Fern K. Willits, and Conrad L. Kanagy, "Rurality and Well-Being During the Middle Years of Life," *Social Indicators Research*, May 1991. And importantly,

the newer studies don't claim to demonstrate *causality*, that is, that people in rural areas are happier *because* they live where they do.

[48]Brad Roth, *God's Country: Faith, Hope and the Future of the Rural Church* (Harrisonburg, VA: Herald Press, 2017), 34.

3. WHY SMALL PLACES ARE WORSE THAN WE THINK

[1]Alice Lyons, "All Country Roads Lead to Rome: Idealization of the Countryside in Augustan Poetry and American Country Music," *CMC Senior Theses* 102 (spring 2011): 103, www.scholarship.claremont.edu/cmc_theses/102.

[2]See Lyons, "All Country Roads".

[3]Lyons, "All Country Roads," 8.

[4]J. D. Vance, *Hillbilly Elegy* (New York: Harper, 2016), 20.

[5]Kathleen Norris, *Dakota* (New York: Houghton Mifflin Harcourt, 2001), 50, 59.

[6]Robert Wuthnow, *Small-Town America* (Princeton, NJ: Princeton University Press, 2015), xii.

[7]Eliza Southgate, *A Girl's Life Eighty Years Ago* (New York: Charles Scribner's, 1887), 100, https://archive.org/stream/agirlslifeeight00cookgoog#page/n140/mode/2up.

[8]Victor Davis Hanson, "The Oldest Divide," *City Journal*, autumn 2015, www.city-journal.org/html/oldest-divide-14042.html.

[9]Calvin Beale, *A Taste of the Country*, ed. Peter A. Morrison (University Park: Pennsylvania State University Press, 1990), 10.

[10]Patrick J. Carr and Maria J. Kefalas, *Hollowing Out the Middle: The Rural Brain Drain and What It Means for America*, 2nd ed. (Boston: Beacon, 2010), 76.

[11]Wendell Berry, *Jayber Crow* (Washington, DC: Counterpoint, 2000), 139.

[12]Wuthnow, *Small-Town America*, 104.

[13]See, e.g., Joan Williams, "What So Many People Don't Get About the U.S. Working Class," *Harvard Business Review*, November 10, 2016, https://hbr.org/2016/11/what-so-many-people-dont-get-about-the-u-s-working-class.

[14]See Robert Wuthnow, *The Left Behind: Decline and Rage in Rural America* (Princeton, NJ: Princeton University Press, 2018), 46.

[15]Wuthnow, *Left Behind*, 53; and Wuthnow, *Small-Town America*, 79-82.

[16]Between 1980 and 2000, seven hundred rural counties in the United States lost 10 percent or more of their population. See Carr and Kefalas, *Hollowing*

Out, 2. And between 2000 and 2015, thirteen hundred rural counties experienced population loss. See David B. Danbom, *Born in the Country*, 2nd ed. (Baltimore, MD: Johns Hopkins University Press, 2006), 249.

[17]Alan Smith and Jill Hopkinson, eds., *Faith and the Future of the Countryside* (Norwich, UK: Canterbury Press, 2012), xiv-xv.

[18]Danbom, *Born in the Country*, 249.

[19]Wuthnow, *Small-Town America*, 321.

[20]Carr and Kefalas, *Hollowing Out the Middle*, 19, 24.

[21]Steve Donaldson, "The Rural Reality of Poverty," *National Association of Evangelicals*, fall 2017, 20-21, www.nae.net/rural-reality-poverty.

[22]Kenneth Johnson, "Rural America Undergoing a Diversity of Demographic Change," *Population Reference Bureau*, May 1, 2006, www.prb.org/ruralam ericaundergoingadiversityofdemographicchange.

[23]Glenn Daman, *The Forgotten Church: Why Rural Ministry Matters for Every Church in America* (Chicago: Moody Publishers, 2018), 94.

[24]Daman, *Forgotten Church*, 95.

[25]Alan Berube, "America's Male Employment Crisis Is Both Urban and Rural," *Brookings*, December 5, 2016, www.brookings.edu/research/americas-male -employment-crisis-is-both-urban-and-rural.

[26]Haeyoun Park and Matthew Bloch, "How the Epidemic of Drug Overdose Deaths Rippled Across America," *New York Times*, January 19, 2016, www .nytimes.com/interactive/2016/01/07/us/drug-overdose-deaths-in-the-us .html.

[27]Carr and Kefalas, *Hollowing Out the Middle*, 79.

[28]Casey McDermott, "Despite Initial Projections, N.H. Overdose Deaths Didn't Decline in 2017," *New Hampshire Public Radio*, April 20, 2018, www .nhpr.org/post/despite-initial-projections-nh-overdose-deaths-didnt -decline-2017#stream/0; and "New Hampshire Drug Rehabs," Addiction Center, accessed March 7, 2019, www.addictioncenter.com/rehabs/new -hampshire.

[29]Sarah Eekhoff Zylstra, "America's Epidemic: How Opioid Addicts Find Help in the Church," *Gospel Coalition*, August 31, 2017, www.thegospelcoalition .org/article/americas-epidemic-how-opioid-addicts-find-help-in-the -church.

[30]Carr and Kefalas, *Hollowing Out the Middle*, 77.

[31]Arezou Rezvani, Rachel Martin, and Danny Hajek, "A New Wave of Meth Overloads Communities Struggling with Opioids," NPR, June 20, 2018,

www.npr.org/sections/health-shots/2018/06/20/619929939/a-new
-wave-of-meth-overloads-communities-struggling-with-opioids.

[32]"Leading Causes of Death in Nonmetropolitan and Metropolitan Areas—
United States, 1999–2014," CDC, January 13, 2017, www.cdc.gov/mmwr
/volumes/66/ss/ss6601a1.htm.

[33]Elizabeth M. Stein, Keith P. Gennuso, Donna C. Ugboaja, and Patrick L.
Remington, "The Epidemic of Despair Among White Americans: Trends in
the Leading Causes of Premature Death, 1999–2015," *American Journal of
Public Health*, October 2017, https://ajph.aphapublications.org/doi
/pdf/10.2105/AJPH.2017.303941.

[34]See Anne Case and Angus Deaton, "Rising Morbidity and Mortality in
Midlife Among White Non-Hispanic Americans in the 21st Century,"
PNAS, September 17, 2015, www.pnas.org/content/pnas/early/2015/10/29
/1518393112.full.pdf; and Anne Case and Angus Deaton, "Mortality and
Morbidity in the 21st Century," *Brookings*, March 23, 2017, www.brookings
.edu/bpea-articles/mortality-and-morbidity-in-the-21st-century.

[35]Tena Stone, "Rural Matters," Rural Matters Institute Conference, North-
place Church, Sachse, TX, September 19-20, 2017.

[36]Brady E. Hamilton, Lauren M. Rossen, and Amy M. Branum, "Teen Birth
Rates for Urban and Rural Areas in the United States, 2007–2015," *NCHS
Data Brief*, November 2016, www.cdc.gov/nchs/data/databriefs/db264
.pdf.

[37]Vance, *Hillbilly Elegy*, 7.

[38]One of the underlying questions in *Hillbilly Elegy* is the extent to which
white, working-class people ought to be held responsible for their misfor-
tunes. See Jennifer Senior, "Review: In 'Hillbilly Elegy,' a Tough Love Analysis
of the Poor Who Back Trump," *New York Times*, August 10, 2016, www.ny
times.com/2016/08/11/books/review-in-hillbilly-elegy-a-compassionate
-analysis-of-the-poor-who-love-trump.html.

[39]Stein et al., "Epidemic of Despair Among White Americans."

[40]Timothy Keller and Kathy Keller, *The Meaning of Marriage* (New York:
Penguin, 2013), 48.

[41]Joshua Rothman, "The Lives of Poor White People," *New Yorker*, September 12, 2016, www.newyorker.com/culture/cultural-comment/the-lives
-of-poor-white-people.

4. THE SOURCE AND GOAL OF SMALL-PLACE MINISTRY

[1]Richard Lints, *The Fabric of Theology* (Grand Rapids: Eerdmans, 1993), 316.

[2]Timothy Keller, *Center Church: Doing Balanced, Gospel-Centered Ministry in Your City* (Grand Rapids: Zondervan, 2012), 17.

[3]Keller, *Center Church*, 17.

[4]Keller, *Center Church*, 18.

[5]Keller, *Center Church*, 18.

[6]Stephen T. Um and Justin Buzzard, *Why Cities Matter* (Wheaton, IL: Crossway, 2013), 91.

[7]Darrin Patrick and Matt Carter, *For the City* (Grand Rapids: Zondervan, 2010), 75.

[8]Um and Buzzard, *Why Cities Matter*, 87-88.

[9]The Archbishops' Commission on Rural Areas produced the 1990 report *Faith in the Countryside: A Report Presented to the Archbishops of Canterbury and York* (Worthing, UK: Churchman Publishing, 1990). That report was followed by a 2010 conference that produced Alan Smith and Jill Hopkinson, eds., *Faith and the Future of the Countryside* (Norwich, UK: Canterbury Press, 2012). Both volumes reflect theologically while giving attention to the needs of the countryside. Also from an English, non-evangelical perspective, Tim Gibson has rooted his rural theology in the regular practice of the Eucharist. See his *Church and Countryside: Insights from Rural Theology* (London: SCM Press, 2010).

[10]I'm drawing here on Don Carson's essay "What Is the Gospel?—Revisited," in *For the Fame of God's Name: Essays in Honor of John Piper* (Wheaton, IL: Crossway, 2010).

[11]Carson, "What Is the Gospel?—Revisited," 161.

[12]Carson, "What Is the Gospel?—Revisited," 162.

[13]Martin Luther, "Psalm 117," quoted in Thomas R. Schreiner, *Galatians*, Zondervan Exegetical Commentary on the New Testament (Grand Rapids: Zondervan, 2010), 175.

[14]Tim Keller, "The Centrality of the Gospel," New City Church, accessed March 7, 2019, www.newcityindy.org/wp-content/uploads/2011/07/centrality-of-gospel.-keller.pdf.

[15]See Romans 9:22-24; 1 Corinthians 11:2-16; 14:26-33. Paul applies this see-through principle both to his conversion (1 Timothy 1:12-16) and ministry practice (1 Corinthians 9:18).

[16]Barry Danylak, *Redeeming Singleness* (Wheaton, IL: Crossway, 2010), 208.

5. STRATEGIC ISN'T ALWAYS WHAT WE THINK

[1]Ed Stetzer, "5 Future Trends in Church Planting," *Outreach*, May 11, 2016, www.outreachmagazine.com/features/17259-5-future-trends-in-church -planting.html.

[2]Timothy Keller, *Why God Made Cities* (New York: Redeemer City to City, 2013), 34, www.gospelinlife.com/downloads/why-god-made-cities.

[3]Eckhard J. Schnabel, *Early Christian Mission* (Downers Grove, IL: IVP Academic, 2004), 1:383.

[4]Schnabel, *Early Christian Mission*, 2:1330.

[5]Brad Roth, *God's Country: Faith, Hope and the Future of the Rural Church* (Harrisonburg, VA: Herald Press, 2017), 34.

[6]Roth, *God's Country*, 32.

[7]On serving rural seniors, see Albert Jewell, "Older People in the Country: Burden or Blessing?" in *Faith and the Future of the Countryside*, ed. Alan Smith and Jill Hopkinson (Norwich, UK: Canterbury Press, 2012), 136-55.

[8]"Catch the Vision," Village Missions, accessed March 7, 2019, https ://vimeo.com/244707872.

[9]Eugene Peterson, *The Pastor* (New York: HarperCollins, 2012), 224.

[10]Donnie Griggs, *Small Town Jesus* (Damascus, MD: EverTruth, 2016), 48.

6. SMALL IS USUALLY BETTER THAN WE THINK

[1]"Table 2: Continuity and Change in American Congregations: Congregations' Perspective," National Congregations Study, December 2015, www .soc.duke.edu/natcong/Docs/NCSIII_report_final_tables.pdf, 11.

[2]"Size of Congregation," Association of Religion Data Archives, 2012, www .thearda.com/ConQS/qs_295.asp.

[3]Robert Wuthnow, *Small-Town America* (Princeton, NJ: Princeton University Press, 2015), 219.

[4]Glenn Daman, *The Forgotten Church: Why Rural Ministry Matters for Every Church in America* (Chicago: Moody Publishers, 2018), 26.

[5]Daman, *Forgotten Church*, 146.

[6]Richard Sibbes, *The Bruised Reed* (Carlisle, PA: Banner of Truth, 1998), 17.

[7]Wuthnow, *Small-Town America*, 101.

[8]Wuthnow, *Small-Town America*, 124-25.

[9]Donnie Griggs, "3 Challenges of Small-Town Ministry," *Gospel Coalition*, September 1, 2017, www.thegospelcoalition.org/article/3-challenges-of -small-town-ministry.

[10]Wuthnow, *Small-Town America*, 226, 432.

[11]Ron Klassen and John Koessler, *No Little Places* (Grand Rapids: Baker, 1996), 76-79.

[12]E. B. White, *Here Is New York*, 3rd ed. (New York: Little Bookroom, 2000), 22, 33.

[13]Sibbes, *Bruised Reed*, 10.

[14]Timothy Keller, *Making Sense of God* (New York: Penguin, 2018), 208.

[15]On restless patience in the Christian life, see Stephen Witmer, *Eternity Changes Everything* (Surrey, UK: Good Book Company, 2014).

[16]Faith Cook, *William Grimshaw of Haworth* (Carlisle, PA: Banner of Truth, 1997), 28.

[17]J. C. Ryle, *Five Christian Leaders* (Carlisle, PA: Banner of Truth, 1963), 29.

[18]Cook, *William Grimshaw of Haworth*, 54.

[19]John Newton, quoted in Cook, *William Grimshaw of Haworth*, 45.

[20]Ryle, *Five Christian Leaders*, 33.

[21]William Grimshaw, quoted in Ryle, *Five Christian Leaders*, 31.

[22]Cook, *William Grimshaw of Haworth*, 79.

[23]Cook, *William Grimshaw of Haworth*, 66, 125.

[24]Cook, *William Grimshaw of Haworth*, 167.

[25]John Newton, quoted in Cook, *William Grimshaw of Haworth*, 98.

7. SLOW IS OFTEN WISER THAN WE THINK

[1]John Paton, *John G. Paton: Missionary to the New Hebrides*, ed. James Paton (London: Banner of Truth Trust, 1965), 347.

[2]John Paton, *John G. Paton*, 351.

[3]John Paton, *John G. Paton*, 354-55.

[4]John Paton, *John G. Paton*, 358.

[5]John Paton, *John G. Paton*, 200.

[6]John Paton, quoted by F. W. Boreham, *A Casket of Cameos, or, More Texts That Made History* (Philadelphia: Judson Press, 1924), www.wholesome words.org/missions/biopaton7.html.

[7]Robert Wuthnow, *Small-Town America* (Princeton, NJ: Princeton University Press, 2015), 59-60.

[8]Wuthnow, *Small-Town America*, 55.

[9]Wuthnow, *Small-Town America*, 403.

[10]Wuthnow, *Small-Town America*, 56.

[11]Brad Roth, *God's Country: Faith, Hope and the Future of the Rural Church* (Harrisonburg, VA: Herald Press, 2017), 111.

[12]Wendell Berry, *Jayber Crow* (Washington, DC: Counterpoint, 2000), 160.

[13]Ron Klassen and John Koessler, *No Little Places* (Grand Rapids: Baker, 1996), 39.

[14]Wuthnow, *Small-Town America*, 178.

[15]Wuthnow, *Small-Town America*, 179.

[16]Roth, *God's Country*, 64.

[17]Roth, *God's Country*, 54.

8. FRUITFUL SMALL-PLACE MINISTRY

[1]Robert Wuthnow, *Small-Town America* (Princeton, NJ: Princeton University Press, 2015), 341.

[2]Wuthnow, *Small-Town America*, 361.

[3]Wuthnow, *Small-Town America*, 52-53.

[4]Wuthnow, *Small-Town America*, 57-58.

[5]E. B. White, "Here Is New York" in *Essays of E. B. White* (New York: Harper, 2006), 156-57.

[6]Brian Alexander, "What America Is Losing as Its Small Towns Struggle," *Atlantic*, October 18, 2017, www.theatlantic.com/business/archive/2017/10/small-town-economies-culture/543138.

[7]Wuthnow, *Small-Town America*, 363.

[8]Wuthnow, *Small-Town America*, 362.

[9]Wuthnow, *Small-Town America*, 357.

[10]Wuthnow, *Small-Town America*, 78.

[11]National Association of Evangelicals, quoted in Harold Longenecker, *Building Town and Country Churches: A Practical Approach to the Revitalization of Churches* (Chicago: Moody Press, 1973), 27.

[12]Leith Anderson, quoted in Glenn Daman, *The Forgotten Church: Why Rural Ministry Matters for Every Church in America* (Chicago: Moody Publishers, 2018), 151.

[13]Paul Jorgensen, "On Pastoring the Rural," National Association of Evangelicals, fall 2017, 25, www.nae.net/on-pastoring-the-rural.

[14]Winn Collier, *Love Big, Be Well: Letters to a Small Town Church* (Grand Rapids: Eerdmans, 2017), 135.

[15]Wuthnow, *Small-Town America*, 125.

[16]See Aaron Morrow, *Small Town Mission* (n.p.: GCD Books, 2016).

[17]Daman, *Forgotten Church*, 86.

[18]J. C. Ryle, *Five Christian Leaders* (Carlisle, PA: Banner of Truth, 1963), 32.

[19]Ron Klassen and John Koessler, *No Little Places* (Grand Rapids: Baker, 1996), 48, 68.

[20]Cf. Donnie Griggs, *Small Town Jesus* (Damascus, MD: EverTruth, 2016), 115-19, 140-41.

[21]Robert Wuthnow, *The Left Behind: Decline and Rage in Rural America* (Princeton, NJ: Princeton University Press, 2018), 151-56; and J. D. Vance, *Hillbilly Elegy* (New York: Harper, 2016), 7, 163.

[22]Daman, *Forgotten Church*, 86; and Wuthnow, *Small-Town America*, 112.

[23]Faith Cook, *William Grimshaw of Haworth* (Carlisle, PA: Banner of Truth, 1997), 58.

9. BATTLING JOY KILLERS IN SMALL-PLACE MINISTRY

[1]John Drury, *Music at Midnight: The Life and Poetry of George Herbert* (New York: Penguin Books, 2013), 209-14.

[2]George Herbert, *The Complete English Works*, ed. Ann Pasternak Slater (London: Everyman's Library, 1995), 361.

[3]Herbert, *Complete English Works*, 219.

[4]Herbert, *Complete English Works*, 359-60.

[5]Winn Collier, *Love Big, Be Well: Letters to a Small-Town Church* (Grand Rapids: Eerdmans, 2017), 102.

[6]Collier, *Love Big, Be Well*, 54.

[7]Herbert, *Complete English Works*, 234.

[8]Herbert, *Complete English Works*, 199.

[9]Herbert, *Complete English Works*, 200.

[10]Herbert, *Complete English Works*, 220.

[11]Thomas Watson, *The Godly Man's Picture* (Edinburgh: Banner of Truth, 1992), 81.

[12]These seven strategies for fighting envy are lightly adapted from Stephen Witmer, "Seven Strategies for Fighting Envy," *Desiring God* (blog), July 1, 2018, www.desiringgod.org/articles/seven-strategies-for-fighting-envy.

[13]John Brown, quoted in Mark Dever, *What Is a Healthy Church?* (Wheaton, IL: Crossway, 2007), 36-37.

[14]Brad Roth, *God's Country: Faith, Hope and the Future of the Rural Church* (Harrisonburg, VA: Herald Press, 2017), 183-84.

10. GOOD AND BAD REASONS NOT
TO DO SMALL-PLACE MINISTRY

[1]Wendell Berry, "God and Country," in *What Are People For?* (Berkeley, CA: Counterpoint, 2010), 97.

[2]Mark T. Mulder and James K. A. Smith, "Subdivided by Faith? An Historical Account of Evangelicals and the City," *Christian Scholar's Review* 38 (2009).

[3]Glenn Daman, *The Forgotten Church: Why Rural Ministry Matters for Every Church in America* (Chicago: Moody Publishers, 2018), 26.

[4]Allan Barth, "A Vision for Our Cities," *City to City* (blog), January 1, 2009, www.redeemercitytocity.com/blog/a-vision-for-our-cities.

[5]David Brooks, "I Dream of Denver," *New York Times*, February 16, 2009, www.nytimes.com/2009/02/17/opinion/17brooks.html.

[6]Timothy Keller, *Why God Made Cities* (New York: Redeemer City to City, 2013), 21, www.gospelinlife.com/downloads/why-god-made-cities.

[7]Robert Wuthnow, *Small-Town America* (Princeton, NJ: Princeton University Press, 2015), 72-74.

[8]Sarah Pulliam Bailey, "Some Evangelicals Question Whether They Have Overlooked the Rural Church," *Washington Post*, December 15, 2016, www.washingtonpost.com/news/acts-of-faith/wp/2016/12/15/some-evangelicals-question-whether-they-have-overlooked-the-rural-church/?utm_term=.3c13780d0388.

[9]Darren Carlson, "God Loves My Boring, Unimportant Neighborhood," *Gospel Coalition*, August 29, 2014, www.thegospelcoalition.org/article/god-loves-my-boring-unimportant-neighborhood.

[10]Eugene Peterson, *The Pastor* (New York: HarperCollins, 2012), 224-25.

[11]Boris Johnson, quoted in Carl Swanson, "105 Minutes with Boris Johnson," *New York Magazine*, June 15, 2012, http://nymag.com/news/intelligencer/encounter/boris-johnson-2012-6.

[12]J. C. Ryle, *Five Christian Leaders* (Carlisle, PA: Banner of Truth, 1963), 25.

[13]Timothy Keller, *Center Church: Doing Balanced, Gospel-Centered Ministry in Your City* (Grand Rapids: Zondervan, 2012), 165.

[14]John Starke, "Planting a Church Is Lonely," *Gospel Coalition*, January 8, 2018, www.thegospelcoalition.org/article/planting-church-lonely.

11. GOOD AND BAD REASONS TO DO SMALL-PLACE MINISTRY

[1]Robert Wuthnow, *Small-Town America* (Princeton, NJ: Princeton University Press, 2015), 127.

[2]Donnie Griggs, "Is God Calling You to Go Home?" *Gospel Coalition*, February 21, 2018, www.thegospelcoalition.org/article/god-calling-you-go-home.

[3]Ron Klassen and John Koessler, *No Little Places* (Grand Rapids: Baker, 1996), 45.

[4]Cf. Eugene Peterson, *The Pastor* (New York: HarperCollins, 2012), 225.

[5]Glenn Daman, *The Forgotten Church: Why Rural Ministry Matters for Every Church in America* (Chicago: Moody Publishers, 2018), 47.

[6]Daman, *Forgotten Church,* 47.

[7]Tish Harrison Warren, "I Overlooked the Urban Poor—Then Trump Came Along," *Christianity Today*, August 22, 2016, www.christianitytoday.com /ct/2016/september/i-overlooked-rural-poor-then-trump-came-along .html.

[8]Patricia M. Y. Chang, *Assessing the Clergy Supply in the 21st Century* (Durham, NC: Duke Divinity School, 2004), 2, www.pulpitandpew.org /assessing-clergy-supply-21st-century.html.

[9]David Van Biema, "Rural Churches Grapple with a Pastor Exodus," *Time*, January 29, 2009, http://content.time.com/time/magazine/article/0,9171 ,1874843,00.html.

[10]Daman, *Forgotten Church*, 197-98.

[11]Daman, *Forgotten Church*, 226.

[12]Timothy Keller, "Are You Saying That All Churches Should Make Cities a Priority?" *Gospel Coalition*, March 31, 2010, www.thegospelcoalition.org /article/are-you-saying-that-all-christians-should-make-cities-a-priority. Cf. Timothy Keller, *Center Church: Doing Balanced, Gospel-Centered Ministry in Your City* (Grand Rapids: Zondervan, 2012), 166.

[13]Wuthnow, *Small-Town America*, 8, 10.

[14]Tim Gibson, *Church and Countryside: Insights from Rural Theology* (London: SCM Press, 2010), 91-92.

[15]Kathleen Norris, *Dakota* (New York: Houghton Mifflin Harcourt, 2001), 56.

[16]Martin Giese, "The Thriving Rural Church," *National Association of Evangelicals*, fall 2017, www.nae.net/thriving-rural-church.

[17]Timothy Keller, "Why Live in the Big City," *Redeemer Report*, May 2001, 2, https://mcpratt.files.wordpress.com/2010/09/why_live_in_the_big_city .pdf.

12. COMMON REASONS TO PRIORITIZE BIG-PLACE MINISTRY

[1]See Marcus Nodder, *City Lives* (Youngstown, OH: 10 Publishing, 2018); and Mark R. Gornik and Maria Liu Wong, *Stay in the City* (Grand Rapids: Eerdmans, 2017).

[2]E.g. Tim Keller, "The Country Parson," *Gospel Coalition*, December 2, 2009, www.thegospelcoalition.org/article/the-country-parson.

[3]Timothy Keller, *Center Church: Doing Balanced, Gospel-Centered Ministry in Your City* (Grand Rapids: Zondervan, 2012), 21.

[4]See Timothy Keller, "Are You Saying That All Churches Should Make Cities a Priority?" *Gospel Coalition*, March 31, 2010, www.thegospelcoalition.org /article/are-you-saying-that-all-christians-should-make-cities-a-priority.

[5]Timothy Keller, *Why God Made Cities* (Redeemer City to City, 2013), 27, www.gospelinlife.com/downloads/why-god-made-cities.

[6]John L Thompson, *Urban Impact* (Eugene, OR: Wipf and Stock, 2011), 22.

[7]Eckhard J. Schnabel, *Early Christian Mission* (Downers Grove, IL: IVP Academic, 2004), 1:227.

[8]Schnabel, *Early Christian Mission*, 1:383.

[9]Harvie M. Conn and Manuel Ortiz, *Urban Ministry* (Downers Grove, IL: IVP Academic, 2001), 120-21; and Schnabel, *Early Christian Mission*, 1:180.

[10]Schnabel, *Early Christian Mission*, 1:184.

[11]Donnie Griggs, *Small Town Jesus* (Damascus, MD: EverTruth, 2016), 40.

[12]Schnabel, *Early Christian Mission*, 2:1544; Schnabel, *Early Christian Mission*, 1:443.

[13]Thomas A. Robinson, *Who Were the First Christians? Dismantling the Urban Thesis* (New York: Oxford University Press, 2016), 98-99.

[14]Eckhard J. Schnabel, *Paul the Missionary* (Downers Grove, IL: IVP Academic, 2008), 58-59.

[15]Schnabel, *Paul the Missionary*, 285.

[16]Schnabel, *Early Christian Mission*, 1:912.

[17]Schnabel, *Early Christian Mission*, 1:739.

[18]Schnabel, *Early Christian Mission*, 2:1067, n. 152.

[19]Cf. Schnabel, *Paul the Missionary*, 285.

[20]Cf. Acts 13:48-49.

[21]Robinson, *Who Were the First Christians?* 96.

[22]Morna Hooker and Francis Young, *Holiness and Mission: Learning from the Early Church About Mission in the City* (London: SCM Press, 2010), 33.

[23]Robinson, *Who Were the First Christians?* 95.

[24]See Schnabel, *Early Christian Mission*, 2:1300.

[25]E.g., John Stott, *The Message of Romans*, Bible Speaks Today (Downers Grove, IL: InterVarsity Press, 1994), 382; and Thomas R. Schreiner, *Romans*,

Baker Exegetical Commentary on the New Testament (Grand Rapids: Baker, 2018), 770.

[26]Keller, *Why God Made Cities*, 27; Keller, *Center Church*, 154.

[27]Timothy Keller, "Why Live in the Big City," *Redeemer Report*, May 2001, 1-2, https://mcpratt.files.wordpress.com/2010/09/why_live_in_the_big_city .pdf; Allan Barth, "A Vision for Our Cities," *City to City* (blog), January 1, 2009, www.redeemercitytocity.com/blog/a-vision-for-our-cities.

[28]Schnabel, *Paul the Missionary*, 282, 287.

[29]See Robinson, *Who Were the First Christians?* 98; see also 107-21.

[30]Schnabel, *Paul the Missionary*, 281-82.

[31]Schnabel, *Paul the Missionary*, 281.

[32]Schnabel, *Paul the Missionary*, 282-84.

[33]Robinson, *Who Were the First Christians?* 100-102.

[34]Robinson, *Who Were the First Christians?* 102-4.

[35]Robinson, *Who Were the First Christians?* 104-5.

[36]E.g. Barth, "Vision for Our Cities," 2.

[37]Rodney Stark, *Cities of God: The Real Story of How Christianity Became an Urban Movement and Conquered Rome* (New York: HarperCollins, 2006), 26.

[38]E.g., Philip Comfort says Christian churches existed in rural Middle Egypt as early as 125 AD. On the evidence of early rural Christianity, see Robinson, *Who Were the First Christians?* 152-75.

[39]See Robinson, *Who Were the First Christians?* 146-51, from which I've drawn the examples that follow.

[40]Clement of Rome, *1 Clement*, 42:4.

[41]Pliny, *To the Emperor Trajan*, 46.

[42]Justin Martyr, *Dialogue with Trypho*, 118.

[43]Justin Martyr, *First Apology*, 67.

[44]Schnabel, *Early Christian Mission*, 1:598.

[45]Schnabel, *Early Christian Mission*, 2:1570.

[46]Jon M. Dennis, *Christ and City* (Wheaton, IL: Crossway, 2013), 179.

[47]Stephen T. Um and Justin Buzzard, *Why Cities Matter* (Wheaton, IL: Crossway, 2013), 18-19.

[48]Barth, "A Vision for Our Cities," 2. Cf. Um and Buzzard, *Why Cities Matter*, 15; Keller, "Why Live in the Big City," 1; Keller, *Why God Made Cities*, 34; Keller, *Center Church*, 148, 161.

[49]Keller, *Center Church*, 149; Dennis, *Christ and City*, 175.

[50]Keller, *Center Church*, 150, 149.

[51]Chad Shearer, "The Small Town-Big City Split That Elected Donald Trump," *Brookings*, November 11, 2016, www.brookings.edu/blog/the-avenue /2016/11/11/the-small-town-big-city-split-that-elected-donald-trump.

[52]John Kron, quoted in Glenn Daman, *The Forgotten Church: Why Rural Ministry Matters for Every Church in America* (Chicago: Moody Publishers, 2018), 34.

[53]Um and Buzzard, *Why Cities Matter*, 44; and Keller, *Center Church*, 167.

[54]Richard Florida, quoted in Um and Buzzard, *Why Cities Matter*, 45; and Edward Glaeser, quoted in Dennis, *Christ and City*, 22.

[55]McKinsey Global Institute, "Urban World: Mapping the Economic Power of Cities," March 2011, quoted in Um and Buzzard, *Why Cities Matter*, 125. Cf. Dennis, *Christ and City*, 19; Robert Wuthnow, *Small-Town America* (Princeton, NJ: Princeton University Press, 2015), 402. As we saw earlier, it's true that some people move from city to country, that population shifts from rural to urban have varied over time, and that population gain or loss varies widely between and among rural areas. Cf. Kenneth Johnson, "Rural America Undergoing a Diversity of Demographic Change," *Population Reference Bureau*, May 1, 2006, www.prb.org/ruralamericaundergoingadiversi tyofdemographicchange.

[56]Wuthnow, *Small-Town America*, 320, 335.

[57]See Joel Kotkin, "Why America's Young and Restless Will Abandon Cities for Suburbs," *Forbes*, July 20, 2011, www.forbes.com/sites/joelkotkin /2011/07/20/why-americas-young-and-restless-will-abandon-cities-for -suburbs/#5d4c81843686.

[58]Um and Buzzard, *Why Cities Matter*, 31; Keller, *Center Church*, 159.

[59]Keller, *Center Church*, 20.

[60]Roland Allen, *Missionary Methods* (Abbotsford, WI: Life Sentence, 2017), 12, 17.

[61]Wuthnow, *Small-Town America*, 127.

[62]John Kron, quoted in Daman, *Forgotten Church*, 34.

[63]Victor Davis Hanson, "The Oldest Divide," *City Journal*, autumn 2015, www .city-journal.org/html/oldest-divide-14042.html.

[64]Keller, *Center Church*, 155.

[65]E.g., Dennis, *Christ and City*, 32-34.

[66]E.g., Roger Greenway and Timothy M. Monsma, *Cities: Missions' New Frontier* (Grand Rapids: Baker, 2000), 27, quoted in Timothy Keller, *Why God Made Cities*, 9.

[67]E.g., Barth, "A Vision for Our Cities," 3.

[68]E.g., Um and Buzzard, *Why Cities Matter*; Keller, *Center Church*, 150-51. However, Keller seems again to distinguish between urban and rural in *Center Church* (p. 51), and *Why God Made Cities* (p. 8) mentions only a future city.

[69]Hooker and Young, *Holiness and Mission*, 21, 24.

[70]Brad Roth, *God's Country: Faith, Hope and the Future of the Rural Church* (Harrisonburg, VA: Herald Press, 2017), 211.

[71]Roth, *God's Country*, 215.

CONCLUSION

[1]Marilynne Robinson, *Gilead* (New York: Picado, 2004), 247.

ACKNOWLEDGMENTS

[1]Stephen Witmer, "To Faithful Pastors in Forgotten Places," *Desiring God*, August 27, 2017; Stephen Witmer, "The Secret Small Churches Know Best," *Desiring God*, January 21, 2018; Stephen Witmer, "To the Next Generation of Church Leaders: Three Reasons to Think Bigger than Big," *Desiring God*, March 3, 2018; Stephen Witmer, "Ministry in Small Towns: Worth a Lifetime Investment," *Gospel Coalition*, February 6, 2018; Stephen Witmer, "A Fictional Pastor Teaches Us to Love Big in Small Places," *Gospel Coalition*, March 7, 2018; and Stephen Witmer, "Two (Book) Attempts to Understand Rural America," *Gospel Coalition*, June 25, 2018.

Small Town Summits

Small Town Summits are small, local, affordable gatherings designed to provide support, training, encouragement, and connection for those who long to see God's glory spread throughout the small places of New England.

Much of New England lies beyond the cities. To reach this region for Christ, many gospel workers must live and minister in the small places. We want to encourage and equip these faithful ministers. We don't disdain the big conferences in the big cities with the well-known speakers (on the contrary, we attend and benefit from them). But our Summits are a bit different. We intentionally go small: small conferences in small places for small-town Christian workers. The term "summit" commonly describes a gathering of leaders for the purpose of making significant decisions. Our Small Town Summits gather laypeople, pastors, and ministry leaders within a state or region. We learn from one another as we pray and plan for gospel advance. We worship together, eat together, talk together, learn together, and pray together.

The goal of Small Town Summits is to see the small places of New England filled with healthy, missional, gospel-centered churches and Christian workers, for the glory of God.

smalltownsummits.com

IVP PRAXIS
EQUIPPING LEADERS FOR MINISTRY

"...TO EQUIP HIS PEOPLE FOR WORKS OF SERVICE,
SO THAT THE BODY OF CHRIST MAY BE BUILT UP."

EPHESIANS 4:12

God has called us to ministry. But it's not enough to have a vision for ministry if you don't have the practical skills for it. Nor is it enough to do the work of ministry if what you do is headed in the wrong direction. We need both vision *and* expertise for effective ministry. We need *praxis*.

Praxis puts theory into practice. It brings cutting-edge ministry expertise from visionary practitioners. You'll find sound biblical and theological foundations for ministry in the real world, with concrete examples for effective action and pastoral ministry. Praxis books are more than the "how to" – they're also the "why to." And because *being* is every bit as important as *doing*, Praxis attends to the inner life of the leader as well as the outer work of ministry. Feed your soul, and feed your ministry.

If you are called to ministry, you know you can't do it on your own. Let Praxis provide the companions you need to equip God's people for life in the kingdom.

www.ivpress.com/praxis